LAW SCHOOL CHRONICLES

KENNEY HEGLAND

ISBN: 1534969373
ISBN 13: 9781534969377

LAW SCHOOL CHRONICLES

Professor Hegland is known for clarity, humor, and occasional insight. You'll learn a great deal about law, legal education, and lawsuits. He's an expert. His *Introduction to the Study and Practice of Law* introduces students to law study, and his *Trial and Lawyering Skills* and *A Short and Happy Guide to Being a Lawyer* introduce lawyers to practice.

He has also written *A Short and Happy Guide to Elder Law*. His videos for high school students are distributed by *Discovery* and his short videos on elder law are available at www.Heglandlaw.com.

He has taught at Arizona, UCLA, the University of San Diego, and Harvard. His degrees from Stanford, Berkeley and Harvard prove you can fool some universities, some of the time, and that's good enough for tenure.

Finalist, Tucson Festival of Books

Many important and (in my opinion) correct observations. Chief Justice Thomas Zlaket, Arizona Supreme Court, retired.

Clean, crisp and insightful with humor, pathos, and practical wisdom. Robert Shannon, MD, Director Palliative Care, Mayo Clinic, Jacksonville

Law Students comment:
One of the best books I have ever read. It is short but immensely strong.

The very first page of the book set the tone for the entire read. The "we're dropping like ourselves" joke, followed by "not scheduling hair cuts and car lubes on the same day' were so clever, light-hearted and fun, despite the serious subjects to come.

The sections of the book that talked about law students' experiences were spot on.

A great way for me to reflect on my decision to come to law school and to think about the serious questions I have, from what will practice be like to how will I handle stress and ethical dilemmas.

I wish I read this book as a first-year student.

It was like being a spectator to the thought processes of this very lively narrator. I enjoyed following along with the litigation, observations about the politics of academia, and tidbits about legal history.

I learned more about how to think like a lawyer, how to try a lawsuit, than in any course I have taken.

A valuable read for both legal professionals and lay-people.

While I was reading the book I realized how attractive the law is and how much I love it.

For lawyers,
In good times, great jokes,
In bad, great friends.

CHAPTER ONE

I SHOULD GET my affairs in order. Talk to the kids.

Parents' generation, kaput or nearly so. Now movie stars, jocks, friends, high school heartthrobs. The cartoon shows a window-sill, several dead flies, a survivor laments, "We're dropping like ourselves."

But I'm too busy to get to all that paperwork. Sure, time's winged chariot hurrying near and all of that but I'm feeling pretty good. Keeping busy. Teaching one class, a few lectures, a little writing, working on a book. Not scheduling haircuts and car lubes the same day. Health is fine, only four prescriptions – no doubt violating the Golden Rule, taking pleasure hearing colleagues take more pills, higher doses. There's a German word for it, one I never could pronounce much less spell. There's red wine and dark chocolate. Doctor's orders. My wife, Vicki, is diabetic and not amused. I believe Orwell said, celebrating his literary success, two glasses good, four glasses better.

I was (am) a law professor. Boring choice. My daughter Gina's a cop. Every week she has more excitement, more breath-taking intensity, than I have in a year. Not necessarily bank robberies and hostage situations, although there're some of those, but daily interaction with people, events, sometimes threatening, sometimes funny. A couple of nights ago she stopped a car, the driver a skinny kid, goatee, T shirt, well tatted. No passengers, no need to pose. Even before "May I see your driver's license," he meekly offered, "The marijuana in the back seat isn't mine and neither is the cocaine in the trunk."

And Gina gets to ride in the helicopter.

Not that law teaching is without drama. Tenure fights get heated. And there is the brewing fight to allow students to graduate in two years, not three. This promises nasty, yet restrained, memos. The life of the mind generally avoids four-letter words, especially in emails (which can, regrettably, be forwarded to the person you were discussing). But still it's mostly 'Should Constitutional Law be a first-year or a second-year course?' – not exactly staring down a barrel.

I have a corner office thanks to a few early retirements and a most unfortunate coronary. The view is terrific, out across the main quad, green grass, trees, undergraduates lying in groups, talking philosophy, revolution, beer runs. It took me a long time to join the computer age but now I have two screens, one to work on articles, the other to read breaking news and emails from long lost high school friends. How did I even get along with those guys?

Last week I went to a funeral; it put me in something of a funk. The decedent's son stood before the flag draped casket; two Marines in dress uniforms. The Church was quiet save for the soft sobs of the widow.

"Dad dropped out of high school. Hung out, got into a little trouble, but ended up opening a shirt factory in Brooklyn. Did well for several years. When it finally went broke, he joined the merchant marines and spent three years in Burma in the import/export business. When the war broke out he joined the Marines. He got a Silver Star. Didn't talk much about it except that he went to war on the Queen Mary. After the war, he met my mother and opened a corner grocery store. Later he managed the Safeway stores in town."

Funerals. Morbid recognition. I thought of my eulogy.

"Dad graduated high school, never got into real trouble. After college he went to law school and after practicing a little he became a law professor and wrote some articles. He died last week."

No Burma. No Silver Star. No Queen Mary.

Maybe I should have done something different. I've been happy, content, perhaps too content. No need to change jobs, start businesses, take chances. Maybe I should cash out, try something different, open a vineyard, take award-winning photographs, hike the Alps. Aging movie stars, who looked better thirty years ago, assure me that those worlds are still open to me if I would only use the right stockbroker. Obliviously they didn't, squinting at large-font teleprompters and angering the crew with countless retakes.

The phones rings.

"Dad, I got a big case! Wrongful death!"

Wrongful death? Jamie? I pause, look at the ceiling, and hate to be the teacher on the playground but …

"Jamie, hold on! You're a criminal lawyer. You don't do wrongful death cases."

"That's why I'm calling. I'll need your help."

Jamie is my other daughter. When she and Gina played cops and robbers she was always the robber. Vicki and I, remaking the world as do most parents, gave our young daughters trucks, cars, and Lincoln Logs. Alas, they learned too quickly; they wanted guns. Like most parents we stood our ground.

"OK, but only squirt guns that *don't* make machine gun sounds and, yes, jelly donuts on the way home but only this once." (They really aren't that bad for you if you only have two.)

Jamie grew up wanting to be a public defender, protecting the innocent and, if not the innocent, the Constitution. After a couple of years she opened her own office. Cracking the monthly nut is hard work. She employs two lawyers, Rachael and Bill, an investigator, George, and two secretaries (now "legal assistants," thank you very much). Not to mention rent on the spiffy downtown office, new IPhones and computers, bar dues and mandatory Continuing Legal Education courses. Fortunately malpractice insurance is not high for criminal defense lawyers. Dissatisfied clients are in prison and "I got ten years for shooting that bastard but if my lawyer hadn't screwed up I would have got only seven" doesn't have great jury appeal.

"Dad, I just spent an hour with them. I explained I do criminal law and not wrongful death. But they insisted. I got his brother off on an extreme DUI and he swears by me. They'll be in tomorrow to sign the retainer."

"Civil is a lot different than criminal. Depositions, interrogatories, motions for summary judgment."

"I've tried scores of jury trials and am pretty good at it. We can do this. Marie is our client, you'll love her. Derrick Wilson is her guardian. Her mother died in her sleep when the pilot on her gas furnace went out. Marie had spent the night at a friend's house, and the next morning when she walked into their living room, she discovered her mother's body."

"Jesus. How old is she?"

"Thirteen."

Thirteen. To walk in alone and find your mother dead. Fuck.

"They couldn't find any of Marie's relatives so they put her in a group home. It gets worse. She might have been sexually abused by a kid in the home."

Sick humor is how soldiers deal with it; lawyers retreat to the safety of the law where we turn people into plaintiffs and defendants, tragedy into causes of action.

"Who are the defendants?"

"*Everheat* made the furnace and she purchased it at Jack's Appliances."

"Jamie, this sounds like a law school exam."

On that dreaded day, students are given short stories filled with hidden legal issues. Their first task is to find them. Can Marie sue *Everheat?* Jack's Appliances? Under what legal theories and what defenses will she encounter? Can she recover for the sexual assault? Will the court have jurisdiction over an out-of-state defendant?

Once the students spot the issues, they're to discuss the various legal principles that come into play, often vague and sometimes in conflict. Analysis counts, not conclusions. *Getting to Maybe* is a popular book on taking law exams; no wonder you can't get a straight answer from your lawyer.

You might believe law is certain, 'Don't walk on the grass'. But it isn't. Lawyers spot ambiguities. 'Is jogging walking?' 'What if it isn't 100% grass? What if there are weeds?' Even after a great deal of legal research, it'll still be hard to predict how Marie's case will fare. Years ago a British jurist, reeking of wisdom and of pomposity,

"*The law should be certain,*" he paused for effect, "*as certainty leads to repose.*" He no doubt nodded.

Oliver Wendell Holmes, a drummer in the Civil War, a Supreme Court Justice until 1931, and the author of 'a clear and present danger,' knew better:

Certainty is illusion and repose is not the destiny of man.

But why rush in? "I dunno, Jamie. We shouldn't get in over our heads. *Everheat* will get high-powered lawyers."

"Dad, you and mom have encouraged me to bite off more than I can chew. You should too. At least come down tomorrow and meet Marie. Then decide."

Go downtown? Bill, my bridge partner, was on jury duty. The judge asked, "Should I call you Professor Boyd or Mr. Boyd?"

"Mr. Boyd is fine."

"You know, Mr. Boyd, I was in two of your classes. Got a B in one and a C in the other. Knowing that will you do what I tell you, *Professor* Boyd?"

Still, a big time lawsuit might be fun. Jamie will do the trial, I'll just sit there, offering suggestions. And what about what I preach to my students – our highest calling, helping people at critical times. A young girl finds her mother dead.

Parking's always a bitch downtown; if we get a big verdict I can buy a new suit. Get Vicki off my back.

"No promises."

CHAPTER TWO

"I THOUGHT MOM killed herself."

Marie's eyes are dry, her voice steady. I want to jump in, "Oh, you poor thing," reassure her, "It was an accident." Jamie knows better. Let Marie talk, let her get through it, let her say what she needs to say, not what you want to hear.

"You thought your mother killed herself." Jamie hands her a Kleenex and then Marie's voice breaks.

"Yes. Ever since Dad died …. He was a hero. Saved two of the guys in the Humvee before they got him. I have his Purple Heart. On my necklace." She pulls it out, not to show, but to hold. My eyes are no longer dry. "Mom couldn't handle it. Drank."

Marie has short brown hair, average height, and looks younger than 13. Articulate. How can she get through this?

"Marie, I'll be with you." Jamie reaches across the table and takes her hand.

Winning a case is often a crapshoot, what isn't a crapshoot is being with your client, a knowledgeable friend helping them through trying, scary, and often desperate times. "The next hearing is only to set the trial date. You have to be there but don't worry they won't take you to jail."

We're sitting around a small conference table in Jamie's office. No sitting behind an imposing desk for her. Diplomas on the wall, a few paintings from local artists, and the required bookcase filled with impressive law books, books no longer used thanks to the internet. Jamie goes over background stuff. Soccer (goalie), friends (Margot and Kate), school (everything but math), plans (maybe a doctor), best time, reading with her mom (Harry Potter). Finally, "Marie, I understand when you were in the group home there was a boy named Mike Spring."

"Yes." Marie looks down at her hands, hesitates.

"Did anything go on? Did Mike touch you?"

It's extremely difficult to ask children about sexual encounters without leading them to say what they think the interviewer (usually a cop) wants to hear. There are people in prison because of this. But Marie's 13 and this shouldn't be a problem.

Marie answers quickly. "It's not like I was raped or anything. Maybe I led him on. I don't want to get Mike in trouble."

"Don't worry Marie, Mike won't be in trouble unless he did something wrong. Enough for today. I'll call you tomorrow. You have my cell. Call or text anytime, even the middle of the night. We'll get though this."

They hug. We don't teach hugs in law school. I shake hands. Jamie looks over Marie's shoulder; she knows she has me.

I'm not good with people but I'm crackerjacks with issues. We walk to a small hole-in-the-wall café. It's quick and crowded. I order the special, meatloaf, mashed potatoes, gravy, and the mystery vegetables one always gets and never eats.

"*Everheat* might use the drinking to show it was the mom's fault. Could have saved herself if she wasn't drunk."

"Risky to attack the victim," Jamie shakes her head.

"But blaming the victim is what you criminal defense lawyers do." I'm also crackerjacks at clever remarks. Jamie ignores me.

"My concern is how Marie will stand up when they take her depo. No doubt Sullivan and Myers will represent *Everheat* and those bastards will try to destroy her. Remember the Rebecca Cook case?"

"Yeah, sex discrimination. Fuzzy on the details." I signal for more coffee and push my plate, and the uneaten veggies, aside. But mashed potatoes are gone.

"The boss allowed co-workers to post pictures and tell crude blonde jokes. She sued for sex discrimination but dropped the suit after her depo. Sullivan had three male attorneys, the boss, and a male court reporter in the room. Made her recount, in graphic detail, every sexual encounter she had, from grade school on. Where exactly did he touch you?"

"Bull shit. Her lawyers could have protected her," I'm actually pissed, ashamed of my profession. "That doesn't lead to admissible evidence. Tell her not to answer. Walk out. Get a protective order from the judge."

"Dad, that's why you're a professor. In law school depositions are to lead to admissible evidence, in practice they're used to destroy opponents."

Lawyer friends, real lawyers, often gently imply that I don't know anything about "the way it really is." I'll chuckle, good-natured ribbing, nothing more. I want to blurt out "Do too!" … but that would be childish. Yet it stings, more so when it's from the cute little girl you taught 'look both ways'.

"And even if you establish discovery abuse most judges won't do much," adds Rachael. She's Jamie's second hire. Her first, an experienced trial lawyer, couldn't adjust to a younger, less experienced, female boss. Or maybe it was the other way around. In any event Rachael is younger, less experienced and female. They get along famously.

"What about the sexual abuse?" I spot another one.

"Might be hard to hang *Everheat* with that. Hard to see how a bad furnace leads to sexual abuse. Maybe we should sue Child Protective Services for putting her at risk by putting her in an unsafe home." Jamie is finishing her salad leaving nary a piece of lettuce.

"I'll research the question of foreseeability," offers Rachel. "Maybe we can hang *Everheat*. Even if Marie led him on, doesn't matter. She's underage."

"But Mike is too. Probably still a crime but a lesser one." I'm beginning to wonder who'll pick up the check. "Law's one thing but proof's another. If Mike denies it the jury may not believe it happened and, even if it did, she doesn't seem too traumatized. Hard to get a jury to give big bucks for two teens messing around."

"I'll talk to her more, Dad, maybe it was worse than she said. Rape victims often initially deny what happened." There she goes again, Ivory Tower Dad.

Downtown isn't bad, veggies aside. Even got a high-five from a former student and a "Hey Prof." Even if I don't add much it'll be good to pick up some war stories. Students love them and may come to believe I know what I'm talking about assuming the grey hair doesn't cut it.

"I'm in. Give me a cubby. I'll bring my laptop."

I pick up the check. Parents always do.

CHAPTER THREE

I STILL PLAY tennis, gentlemen's doubles. The aggressiveness of youth -- "It was out!" – has become the friendliness of age -- "Too close to call out." Despite my physical prowess the dean decided I'm too old to teach *Sports Law*. A few years ago it was *AIDS Law*, apparently I'm too dull.

Now I teach *Elder Law*. Important course, and not just for lawyers. If you're like me, you have a Living Will but, if you're like me, you don't know where it is or what it says or what it means. Vegetative state? You know you need a Will but haven't gotten around to it. But let me tell you, ready or not, bad times are coming – failing health, disabled relatives, hospice, pulling plugs, to name a few. Getting ready, getting some legal documents, talking to your family, can avoid heartbreak and family feuds. Best gift you can give.

But law school is about more than law; it's also about what kind of lawyers the students will become.

"An employer comes to you and tells you he wants to fire a worker because he's too old," I tell my class. "Is it okay to say 'Age discrimination is against Federal Law and you shouldn't do it but if you do you're likely to get away with it. Age discrimination is hard to prove, few sue, still fewer win, and if they do win, seldom money damages, only reinstatement."

Reader, what do you think?

"You can't tell him that, you're helping the employer break the law."

"No you're not. You are just telling him what the law is. If you don't, the guy down the street will."

"I didn't come to law school to do that sort of thing."

After a few minutes of that back and forth I interject, "You remember Atticus Finch, the lawyer in *To Kill a Mockingbird*. What would he do?" One way to think about ethical problems is to ask what someone you admire would do.

"He's why I came to law school. He'd say 'You can't violate the law and, if you do, I won't represent you.'"

Standing tall with the despised and downtrodden is our profession's proud tradition but it doesn't mean we aren't independent moral actors. In 1836 David Hoffman wrote the first American book on legal ethics.

"I will never plead the Statute of Limitations if my client owes the money. He will never make me a partner in his knavery."

If the lawyer represented the knave it would be malpractice not to raise the defense; however, like Atticus, she need not take his case.

Lawyers were not always mere 'hired guns,' not always simply instruments of their clients' unbridled will. They were pillars of their communities, aristocrats, de Tocqueville observed, who provided order in an otherwise unstable democracy.

Times change, often for the better. The profession is no longer white, Protestant, and male. Supreme Court Justice Sandra Day O'Connor graduated from Stanford in the 60's. She sought work at various law firms, "Sorry, we don't need another secretary."

Pity the lawyer in the still chambers, looking up at her and her fellow Justices.

"Yes, Your Honor, it is true we didn't hire you, Your Honor, but it wasn't just me."

Now about half the law students are women.

And yet: where have you gone, Atticus Finch, a nation turns its lonely eyes to you.

Domestic tranquility is not a given if you have two daughters, roughly the same age, one a cop and the other a defense lawyer. They were such sweet and loving kids until their preteens when they woke up one day suddenly insisting on separate bedrooms, separate friends, and rolling their eyes if Vicki dared to comment on the weather. Being totally out of it, being real old, and, perhaps worst of all, being a man, I seldom offered an opinion and, I regret to admit, usually ducked rather than defend Vicki's assessment of the weather.

Since they have left home and become, thankfully, gainfully employed, their arguments have lost their heat, reduced to occasional bards, Jamie's clients as "scumbags," Gina colleagues as "storm troopers". Gone is the venom on issues that really mattered, like who borrowed whose clothes. Twice a month we have our 'empty nest' dinner where the girls return, mostly to gossip about high school friends, laugh about old arguments, and hear what their parents have been up to (still not very interesting). We live in a middle class neighborhood; years ago most of the law faculty joined the professors of medicine and business in the fancy part of town. We stayed with the underpaid and somewhat resentful professors of history, philosophy, English, anthropology, political science, psychology, all trapped on a sinking boat. But that's another story.

Vicki is a wonderful cook, mostly vegetarian. Toby, our black lab, is mostly disappointed. One topic still generates heat, whether Jamie and I should sue Child Protective Services for placing Marie in an unsafe house. Vicki and Gina recount times they've worked with CPS (Vicki at high school and Gina on the street), how they're good people, overworked, underpaid, doing their best. "It would be criminal to take money needed to help vulnerable kids to line one's pocket with a lawyer fees." Jamie talks of taking on, at great odds, a heartless bureaucracy on behalf of a loving little girl who had been raped.

Toby and I look on.

CHAPTER FOUR

THE TEAM MEETS for breakfast. "Let's decide about Child Protective Services," Jamie takes command. "George, what did you find out about Mike?"

"He's not a bad kid. Went to his old neighborhood. Not well known. A few minor scraps. No rumors about him pushing himself on girls."

George, Jamie's investigator. A retired cop but he's into New Age, Buddhism, or maybe it's Zen. I can never tell which is which. He often drops comments like, "There is no past, no future, only the present moment and now that is gone." These come at the most inappropriate of times, or so it seems to my unenlightened mind, but then again maybe they come at the most appropriate of times. What would Dickens say?

To avoid the lawyer crowd we meet at the 'Rock and Roll Diner'. Posters of Elvis and his guitar, James Dean and his cig, Brando and his cycle, Marilyn and her legs. Red booths, worn with wear, a few white tables, lonely men, down on their luck, at the counter. 'Blue Suede Shoes" plays softly. I pass on the *Woodstock* (bacon and eggs), the *Ringo Starr* (French Toast), and order the *Okie from Muskogee* (pancakes). I love category mistakes.

"Still he could've got carried away. He's at that age." Jamie drops her voice as the waitress approaches.

"Coffee, Dearie?"

Dearie??

Growing old is not for sissies. Death of friends, sickness, falls, and the daily irritants. You're happily living your life, minding your own business, when the AARP letter arrives.

"Greetings!"

Greetings??

Must have confused me with the old guy down the street. Crumble. Trash.

Discouraging looks in the mirror (Dad?) and the crushing day when you get the senior discount without asking. Smiling waitresses who call you "dearie." No longer a player, again a child to be petted, humored.

"Decaf."

I make a point of checking her out, feel young and virile. She smiles but thankfully doesn't pat my head.

"Still you have to feel sorry for Mike," George continues. "He's not in the system for anything he did. His father's in prison, his mother a crack addict."

"He'll never see a real home, from one foster home to another." I'm grim but accurate. "No adoption at his age."

"Should I question him?"

"Dunno, George. You'd be asking him to confess to a crime. Sex registration for life. You'd have to notify his lawyer."

"Mike has a lawyer?" asks Jamie, giving up her diet and reaching for the butter.

Sweet, revenge. "All the kids in Juvenile Court are appointed lawyers. If you didn't spend so much time downtown, daughter dear, you would know that."

I supervise students in the law school's Juvenile Law Clinic. Medical students see patients from the get go. Until the 1970's law students stayed in the library while giants walked the earth.

"We're teaching students to think! As to representing clients and going to court, there's nothing intellectually challenging about it. They'll learn how the first month of practice."

Giants die. (Darwin said that you can never convince your opponents but they eventually die off.) Practical training (often very intellectually challenging) won out. Early clinics represented poor folks; the supervising professors were fresh from Legal Services and Public Defender offices. Heady debates. Was the goal to 'serve the poor' by taking many cases or was it to 'educate the students' by focusing on a few? The early heroes were those who angered legislatures by suing the state or political donors. A threat to defund the law school brought national recognition, a threat to defund the university, made one a rock star.

Things have settled into routine, even hippies run out of energy. Now all law schools have clinics: juvenile and family law clinics, defense and prosecution clinics, environmental law clinics, intellectual property and business planning clinics. Some of our students, who were in the military, are pushing for a Veterans Clinic, wanting to give back to their brothers and sisters. Given limited law school resources, it'll set off a fight.

"OK, let's hold off interviewing Mike." Jamie looks despondently at the hashbrowns. "Maybe we should just call him at trial."

"He'll take the 5th," says Rachael.

"Great, nothing better," Bill is her most recent hire, a cage fighter quick on his feet, seeing questionable, but still legal, moves.

"Marie will testify Mike raped her, we call Mike, he takes the 5th. Game, set, match."

"Was there a rape?" the word sticks in my throat, 'sexual assault' is almost polite. While the fight against sexual exploitation is becoming more public the language is softening. Political correctness where we don't need it.

"Yes. I met with Marie yesterday. It was worse than she first said. I guess she didn't want to talk in front of Granddad."

"Maybe that's what you wanted to hear," I toss back. "And I'm not a granddad." Vicki and I are very proud of our professional daughters and yet there are biological clocks. I'm ready; I still have *Goodnight Moon.*

CHAPTER FIVE

CAN WE SUE Everheat? Marie's mother had no dealing with it, she bought the furnace from the local dealer.

On a fine spring morning in 1909 Donald MacPherson goes motoring in his new Buick. A wheel flies off. Bam! The sound of breaking glass. Donald is bloodied. He sues Buick Motor Company. "The wheel flew off."

Buick is shocked. Outraged actually. "Donald? Donald who? Never heard of no Donald. We didn't sell him no car. He can't sue us. If he has a beef, he can take it up with the local dealer. Have a nice day."

Once that was a good defense. Unless you had face-to-face dealings with someone you couldn't sue them for defective products; in legal talk, you needed 'privity of contract'. Then along came Justice Benjamin Cardozo, one of our profession's Babe Ruths. He changed the rules.

"Go ahead, sue 'em. Best of luck."

A great deal of our law was made up by judges. This is known as 'common law'. Let's back up to happier times. Barnie bought a wagon from Mr. Rubble and later sold it to Fred. Something went wrong with the wagon, what exactly is lost in the mist of time, and Fred sued Mr. Rubble. The Honorable Judge W. Oz threw the case out.

"Fred, you had no dealing with Mr. Rubble so I'm not letting you sue him."

So was born, more or less, the doctrine of privity. Other judges, in similar cases, followed Judge Oz's rule. Following rules previously provides predictability (Mr. Rubble need not worry about strangers) and is a check on judicial bias (judges can't make up new rules to favor their friends). The problem is that times change: what made sense in the local and personal economy of Barnie and Fred makes no sense in the national and corporate world of Buick. So judges can overrule common law doctrines. And that's what Cardozo did. (They can't overrule statutes unless they find them to be unconstitutional.)

"I remember the Buick case," Bill wants us to know he did go to some classes. We're in Jamie's library, table littered with legal pads, laptops, and thankfully cokes and munchies.

"The kid next to me, I think he later dropped out, asked if the injured guy won. The professor stared at him, checked the seating chart, and said with dripping sarcasm, Mr. Harris we just don't care."

All Cardozo said was that he *could* sue Buick; the case went back to the trial court to determine whether the tire was Buick's fault. Who cares? Not us academics. Law school is frustrating. Students learn law from reading appellate cases that raise *legal* issues:

Can a ten year old be sued by his grandmother for pulling out her chair?
Can a nephew inherit from his uncle if he had murdered him?
Can MacPherson sue Buick despite the lack of privity?

Once the legal issue is determined (Maybe, No, Yes) the matter will go back for a trial on the *factual* issues and we never learn what happened. Did he kill the old guy? The court only ruled if he did he shouldn't get the money because "No one should profit from his own wrong!" Of course, on the street *shouldn't* profit and *does* profit are different.

"That case set off a great discussion in Kadish's class," Rachael opens a coke. "Everyone was applauding Cardozo, saying judges that let corporations off lived in the dark ages. But Kadish said they just had a different view of the public good, a different economic theory. It's good when people take chances, build motor cars, and surely there will be occasional accidents. Best to let the loss stay where it falls; otherwise people won't take chances and we'd still be riding horses."

"So this Cardozo fellow caused global warming? Best to shoe your own horse." George again.

"Important debates never go away," the professor in me jumps in. "To encourage new research and innovation, drug companies are given 'safe harbors' from lawsuits if they follow certain procedures. But enough of that. The fact we can sue Everheat doesn't mean we'll win. How can we prove the furnace was defective?"

There is nothing better than sitting around a table talking cases with colleagues.

Thrust: They'll use *Atwood v. Ratner* against us.
Parry: I just read that case. The court stressed the weird facts of that case and suggested its ruling might be limited to those situations. Anyway we can come back with *Henderson*.
Thrust: They'll distinguish *Henderson*.
Parry: I don't think they can. Anyway we still have *Ares v. Massaro*.

Thrust: There was a strong dissent in that case. It might be overruled.

Parry: Remember the case where Rehnquist said he thought *Miranda* was a bad case but voted to affirm it on the basis of precedent?

Thrust: Pass the chips.

In the thickets of the law, cutting bushes, jumping barriers, seeing openings; intensity, excitement, and humor; everyone's on the same side, no one showing off, everyone engaged. George is not impressed.

"They've overrun the Nitpicks, retreat to the Quibbles."

"Maybe we won't have to prove the furnace was defective. Remember the one where the surgeon left a sponge in the woman's stomach?"

Rachael was a star student, Law Review and all of that. Still, given the current market for law grads, she had a hard time getting on with a big civil firm and, with a student debt of over $100,000 (not unusual) she took a job with Jamie. Criminal law -- "I'll never to do that" – seemed to be growing on her; you never can tell.

"I try to forget everything about Torts." Bill was the kind of student who slouched in the back of the room, counting minutes as they stretched into hours. "I never knew how many ways you could be maimed, killed. Almost afraid to go out. What's the sponge got to do with anything?"

"The patient didn't have to prove how the docs screwed up, there was no way the sponge could have been left there unless they did. Maybe we can say the same thing about furnaces going bad."

Much legal argument is by analogy. If we can convince the judge that pilots going out are like forgotten sponges, we won't have to prove negligence.

"Legal theories are fine, maybe we can convince the judge that we don't have to prove negligence but I've seen many fine legal theories crash and burn ... mostly my own." I chuckle at my insincerity. "But unless we can prove *Everheat* screwed up we don't have much of a case."

"We need a smoking gun! Something to inflame the jury," Bill smiles, proud of his pun. "That's George's department."

George's face brakes into an amused expression. "To find the truth, stop looking for it."

"Jesus, George, why can't you be just a retired alcoholic like the rest of your buddies? At least they make sense some of the time."

George nods. "Billy you would have made a good cop. I'll take you with me. We'll talk to local dealers and get some dirt."

CHAPTER SIX

"THE LAW SCHOOL no more belongs in a University than a school of dance."

Thorstein Veblen said that. Or maybe Max Weber, I always get them confused. Law schools had a hard time getting in. Scorned as trade schools, practitioners, not professors, teaching a subject that lacks intellectual interest. In 1870 Christopher Columbus Langdell became the Dean of the Harvard Law School and all of that changed. Damn right law schools belong in the University; law is a science!

"Botanists have their laboratory to discover the basic laws of nature. We have our library to discover the deep principles of law."

Staid academics nodded approval (not to mention university presidents who recognized a cash cow when they saw one – one professor standing before a class of 200).

Lincoln didn't go to law school. He learned as an apprentice. At first law schools were an alternative to apprenticeship. Next step, close down apprenticeships by requiring law school graduation before sitting for the bar. Law professors, never thinking of themselves, argued:

"Lincoln was a lucky exception. Law school training is better. We're thinking of the public good."

This public good became clearer during the great Depression when lawyers, looking over their shoulders, saw a mob of apprenticed lawyers coming their way. "Go back! Spend three years in law school."

At first law schools took anyone who showed up and, after taking their money, flunked them out.

"Look to your right; look to your left; only one of you will be here next year."

Times change. Law schools, now numbering about 180, have become selective, only those with outstanding undergraduate records and a strong showing on admission tests need apply. If Abe had a bad hair day on the LSAT, well, he would've been a wonderful teacher. Now it's:

"Look to your right, look to your left, take a bagel, join the alumni association and make a donation."

As for 'law is a science' it had a good run but no one believes that any more. There are just too many contradictory legal principles, for every tree, a not-tree. What's a poor professor to do? Lecturing is boring and the Socratic Method great fun. No one said law professors are dumb: keep the method but change the goal. It's no longer to learn 'the science of law' or even to learn 'the law' (there's way too much of it). Now the goal is to teach students 'how to think like a lawyer' or, made grandly, 'how to think'.

I spend the afternoon at the law school, sitting in my office, reading about the Oregon Death with Dignity statute; it allows docs to prescribe medicine to end life. Strong philosophical arguments, freedom, being captain of one's ship, having the right to choose. Damn right! But shouldn't everyone have these rights? In Oregon only if you have less than six months to live.

A knock. Our website's proclamation of an 'open door policy' is an aspirational goal, not a promise. Colleagues are walking the halls lobbying the proposal to allow students to graduate early.

"This will allow those who need to begin their careers a year early. We owe them that option. We need your support." I smile and nod.

Knock knock.

"What did Brown want? Hasn't published in decades. No doubt he wants the two-year option. He would be happier in a trade school. Veblen, or maybe it was Weber, was right. We need your support." I smile and nod.

That night Jamie and Gina come to dinner. Vegetable lasagna, salad and wine, red wine. Toby, still a puppy going on four (people) years, is always happy to see me, King of the Food Under the Table. Vickie, according to her doc, a few pounds overweight but she's still quite attractive and her frequent smile always delights.

"Jamie, I'm upset about your saying Marie wouldn't talk about sex in front of granddad." I'm really not but I want to get something in early. Insincerity is better than silence.

Vick moves to her topic – grandkids. "Sometimes I think we raised such accomplished and smart daughters that they scare off men."

"I wish. Go to roll call. They're on you like flies. Pass the lasagna."

"Can't be worse than lawyers. They're convinced that their brains and brawn make them irresistible."

"Your mother found me irresistible even though I had neither."

No one comes to my defense or, for that matter, acknowledges my comment. I don't have much to offer about biological clocks. Jamie is 33, Gina 30. Both look great but they worry about their weight, especially Jamie. First-born perfection. But it's tough living in a world of broccoli and skinless chicken breasts. I pour another glass of wine, think of a few things to say but always a few moments too late. I go to the kitchen in search of pickles. A gracious retreat is better than silence.

"If you win your case you will be taking money better spent on kids in trouble."

Ah, the argument.

"Marie was sexually abused and it's CPS's fault. She should be compensated. And if I lose I will have put in a lot of work and get nothing. Besides if I win the Legislature will realize CPS needs more money and give it to them."

My opening. "Fat chance." But me and the pickles don't make much of an impression. Apparently pickles don't go with lasagna.

"The decision is Marie's. And yes, I told her how hard trials are and how the lawyer for CPS will attack her and make her look bad."

Gina sees her opening.

"Did you tell her how you'll destroy her welfare worker? Make her look incompetent and uncaring, even if she isn't. Maybe Marie likes her and wouldn't want you to do that."

"Trial decisions are for the lawyer. And Gina, can you leave some lasagna?"

Of course with lawyers it's seldom a question of morality; mostly it's "Will it backfire?"

CHAPTER SEVEN

"SHOULD WE SUE Jack's?"

Rachael is drafting our complaint. She's the library lawyer, Bill the street fighter.

"If we join Jack's as a co-defendant we'll have two defendants blaming each other, helping us prove someone was at fault. Fun to watch. But Jack's has the shallow pocket and it would be hard to collect."

Jamie's library. Bill reaches for a coke.

"It's a local store. People know it, maybe shop there, know folks who work there. It'll be a hard sell. If we don't sue them *Everheat* will still say Jack's put in the furnace wrong. We'll come in to defend them. Be local heroes fighting the out-of-state corporation."

"Anyone disagree?"

Silence. "Should we allege the sexual assault?"

"We have a problem, the assault and the bad furnace seem fairly remote."

Protecting wrong doers from crushing liability has been a constant concern. In 1871, on a windy day, Mrs. O'Leary's cow kicks over a lantern and most of Chicago burns. Should Mrs. O'Leary pay to rebuild the city, her cow being judgment proof?

In 1854, on rainy English morning, Hadley takes his broken shaft to Baxendale, the UPS of his day.

"Mate, my mill is shut down, need this shipped for repair immediately."

"No problem, bro. By the end of the week."

Well, there was a problem and Baxendale doesn't get it back for a couple of weeks. Hadley can't open his mill and sues for lost profits. The jury awards him a rather large amount. Baxendale appeals. The appellate judge not only reverses, he fumes.

"Manifest injustice! Wrongdoers must pay for *only* foreseeable losses. Baxendale didn't know Hadley would lose profits."

Despite the American Revolution, our early courts looked to English courts in developing common law. No Sharia law there. *Hadley v. Baxendale* became the best known case in history. As the credits of *Deep Throat* run, the name 'Hadley Baxendale' appears (or so I have been told). It's the ultimate inside joke, although my guess is that folks usually don't stay for the credits.

"If we allege the assault *Everheat* will move to strike it, arguing it wasn't foreseeable under *Hadley*. Then we can't bring it up at trial."

"Come on, Rachael, you were Law Review; you can always make good arguments," Bill's still a tad resentful of law school hierarchy. Success in law school, which rewards basic smarts, does not mean success in practice which rewards common sense, people skills, and gumption. Joe Biden was an average law student and Harry Truman dropped out. There is a wonderful story about a UCLA alumni party in a Malibu villa overlooking the blue Pacific. The owner went over to his Torts professor.

"Remember me, professor? I was in your Torts class." With a sweep of his hand, "This is what a 'D' in Torts gets you."

Bill, who probably slept through ethics, "Let's not bring it up at all and spring it at trial. When Marie testifies, simply have her blurt it out and let them object – can't unring a bell."

That strikes me as sleazy, maybe unethical, but, not wishing to be a moral softie, I keep my thoughts to myself. "Bill, did Tidmore teach you this unring a bell business?"

"Best professor I had." It is actually painful to hear another professor praised.

Bill recognizes his mistake.

"Other than you."

He'll be a good lawyer.

"Tidmore might have overstated this a bit." It is always sweet to suggest, most gently, that a colleague is, well, frankly, incompetent. "Maybe you can't unring a bell but you can silence it. If the judge instructs 'Don't consider the sexual assault,' if one of the jurors brings it up during deliberations the others will shut him down."

"Apples know far more than we realize."

George sees relationships way beyond our ken. Maybe we're watching shadows on cave walls.

"Okay, Bill and I will go seek truth. I got the name of Everheat's regional manager. I'll run into him in a bar. After a few drinks and a little prompting, who knows?"

Is it ethical to have George "run into" Everheat's rep at a bar, lie about who he is, and get harmful statements?

Courts are okay with police lying to defendants: "Your partner has confessed and is blaming you," "We found your fingerprints" or best ever, small interrogation room, defendant handcuffed,

"You shot him."

"Did not. I wasn't even there."

"Not there? Do you know the image of the last person the victim saw stays on his eyes."

Fine and good. But should lawyers' investigators lie?

CHAPTER EIGHT

THERE IS NOTHING better than teaching an engaged class. You walk into the large stadium style auditorium while 120 students settle down. All you have is a seating chart and a list of questions, maybe as many as eight but you seldom use them all. You look around the room, expectant faces, silence falls. You clear your throat.

"Ms. Kettlewell, can you tell us about *Brown v. Finney*?

"Yes. Brown and Finney run into each other in a bar. Finney promises to sell coal to Brown and they shake hands. Later Finney refuses to deliver, claiming he wasn't serious, he was joking."

"And the court held?"

"For Finney. Saying we shouldn't hold people to deals they didn't mean."

"Mr. Cooper, do you agree with the court?"

"Well. Not really. It seems to allow people an easy out after they find they made a bad deal, say they were only joking."

Excellent! Ball in my court. I pace. Class expectant. Should I go practical?

"Mr. Klein, what kind of evidence would you want to show Finney is lying?"

Or should I go theoretical?

"Ms. Adams, what if we really believed Finney was joking and that Brown really believed Finney was serious? Who should win?"

You never know where the class will take you. I've taught *Brown* 30, 35 times but it is never the same. I'm different, the students are different, and even the case is different, every time I read it new things jump out. It's intellectual tennis, the object is not to win the point but to keep the rally going. A few years ago I was at a university dinner, sitting next to the Provost.

"What are goals, the educational outcomes? At the end of an hour, what new knowledge, new skills, new competencies do you want your students to have?"

I was dumbfounded. Not by the question itself but because I never considered it. "Why should we protect jokers? When someone promises you something, should you ask if they are serious? When you make a promise are you conscious of the fact that you may be sued if you don't keep it? If you weren't, should you be held to it?" Not once do I ask myself "What do I want students to learn from the case? What new competency?" As to the rule itself, indeed as to the law, they'll learn that on their own. What do I teach? Questioning.

A friend, a Business School professor, teaches a class with graduate students from various disciplines. "The law students are the best," he told me. Why?

"They ask questions, good questions."

It's a root canal to teach a boring class, to stand before 120 students, some staring blankly, others ignoring you entirely, texting one another or playing computer games. It's humiliating; you ask a provocative, well-thought out question, one which will illustrate an important point. Silence. No hands. No eye contact. You wait an eternity --- was the question that stupid? Am I incomprehensible? Is my fly open? -- and finally you mumble the answer. Occasionally a student jots a note.

When I started teaching, if a student took a note, I was tempted to say "Don't do that, I'm really not that sure." After decades of teaching I am tempted to shout, "You idiots. Write this stuff down. It's important!"

Not all courses are intellectual tennis. Some are boring, at least my Ethics class was. After Watergate where lawyers were bad guys law schools required such courses. They tend to degenerate into pointless and boring debates, with idealists, wringing their hands, "That just isn't right!" and cynics, rubbing their hands, "Paradise can use a little paving."

I invited guest speakers, better them than me. "Talk about some of the ethical problems you've faced."

"When I was just starting out my firm sent me to a trial advocacy program. The faculty was a bunch of hotshot trial lawyers. One said, 'Nothing wrong with telling clients how to dress and I see nothing wrong with dressing up their testimony.' It struck me that the analogy was terrible and that it was unethical. But I didn't say anything. I didn't want to come across as a moral softie."

"We represent an insurance company. One of their insureds caused a horrendous accident, one person killed, another badly injured. We evaluated the case at $3 million. We got a demand from the plaintiff's lawyer, a small town lawyer, for $500,000. We countered with $400,000."

"I do tax law. If you make money illegally you can file a tax return with a number rather than your name. That way the IRS can't call the cops and they can't get you for tax evasion, like they did Al Capone. It's not really an ethical issue, more of an ethical temptation, sitting across from a drug dealer who makes more in a week than I make in a year."

There is a Code of Professional Responsibility. It doesn't tell you how to maintain a tough image, how much you can take advantage of incompetent adversaries, or how to resist Sirens' Song of big bucks and early retirement. (Representing big time druggies isn't a good idea; drug lawyers have been killed by disgruntled clients who apparently didn't realize they could file a bar complaint.)

There are some clear rules. The tax attorney can't tell police what the drug dealer told him; it's confidential. The only time a lawyer can break a confidence is if the client threatens to do future harm. Confessions of past crimes, even where they buried the bodies, are protected.

Jamie always triggers the best discussion. "I can't put on a witness I know will lie. If my client tells me he is guilty, I can't put him on to testify the butler did it. Yet he has a Constitutional right to testify. What should I do?"

"Withdraw if he insists on taking the stand."

"Judges won't let you; they would have to start the trial again."

"Tell your client don't tell me if you did it."

"Yeah, some lawyers do that. But you need to know what happened. Maybe the client thinks he is guilty but has a good defense."

"Put him on the stand and go with his lie."

"A professor wrote an article suggesting that, that your obligation to your client trumps your obligation to the court. He was almost disbarred."

"I saw a movie on TV. The defendant had killed his wife. Before he said anything, the lawyer told him his only chance would be if he was temporarily insane. Then he asked the guy what happened and, sure enough, he was temporarily insane."

"Jimmy Stewart, Anatomy of a Murder. Should've been disbarred for suggesting a winning lie. The hardest thing about being a lawyer is how far you will go to help a client, to make a buck."

Meanwhile, back in the world of illusion, George reports that he and Bill did happen to run into Peter Ulick, *Everheat's* regional manager. After a couple of Margaritas (it's always a couple), Peter expressed hostility toward the company and, yes, he had heard reports of problems with the furnace's pilot.

Good stuff! Ethical issues tend to fade. If lying leads to the truth then lie. But one of my favorite quotes nags.

A man's interest far oftener distorts his judgment than it corrupts his heart.

CHAPTER NINE

"WE'VE DECIDED NOT to sue Jack's Appliances."

"That's nice, dear."

And Vicki accuses *me* of not listening. Still she shows interest in my career, reading my articles, as an English teacher, flagging split infinitives, usually trashing the formal rules. "It's a growing language," she acknowledges. "*Fuck* is the new *gosh*."

High school teachers work harder than law professors, at least according to Vicki. "I'm in the classroom six hours a day, you six hours a week. And I have tests to grade each week, you give one at the end of the semester. And no discipline problems."

"Well, that may be true, dear, but we're paid much more." Vicki's not amused.

In the unlikely event that a state legislator is reading this book, let me assure you that law professors in your state work extremely hard, teaching, writing scholarly articles, supervising clinical students, sitting on community boards, flying to far away conferences.

In addition to teaching Honors English, two English classes, and one poetry class, Vicki supervised the Yearbook, red-lining picture captions like "Sally Jenkins, she actually thought she was cute." Hers was an inner-city school, two out of three faces were black or Hispanic. One year they opened the shipment of yearbooks to find, although the cover was right, the national publisher had switched the contents with that of a high school in Rancho Bernado, a very white school. Her students were shocked but probably not as much as those in sunny California.

"Man, like I know I was stoned the last four years but, dude, I don't recognize *any* of these people."

Her major disappointment: kids, ours included, don't read.

"Give them time. When I was starting my career I was too busy to read novels." Too busy to read novels? Fighting words to an English teacher, but she just smiles at the Neanderthal she married.

Since her retirement, in addition to reading novels, visiting friends, training Toby to be a therapy dog, she volunteers at Hospice. A life changing experience. She has more energy, more enthusiasm, and is happier. She has cut her hair but still colors it. Luckily I notice and compliment.

Vicki seems comfortable with mortality. I'm making progress; I know it's not rage, rage against the fading of the light and I much prefer Dylan's other couplet,

Time held me green and dying,
Though I sang in my chains like the sea.

I still avoid the obituaries and distance the topic with jokes, "I don't mind the idea of dying but I don't want to be there when it happens."

But being there, holding aged hands, comforting the dying, no, being comforted by them, is profound.

"George interviewed a store manager who sells *Everheat* furnaces. Seems they have a hard time installing them and have had complaints. They don't recommend them."

"But no one has died?" Vicki's thankful, our team, disappointed.

"No such luck. The store manager said he complained to the district manager of *Everheat* who blew him off. One step closer to showing they knew."

"That's nice dear." Vicki moves us along. "Reading *Orley Farm* by Trollope, Dickens' contemporary. You know his father was a lawyer?"

"I've read Trollope." He's actually one of my favorites. He writes about people I know (and you would too) and very now and then he stops his story and talks to the reader – 'You may not like Lady Eustance now but wait till the next chapter.' I wish novelists would do more of that. Do you?

"I know you've read Trollope. In *Orley Farm* an old codger marries a young woman. They have a son but the infant is cut out of his will – thus assuring his poverty. The widow forges a codicil putting him back in. Twenty years later, there's a lawsuit. The widow's lawyer knows the truth but knows he can win the case, not by perjury, but by clever lawyering. Should lawyers be loyal to the truth or to their client?"

Lawyers get this question as a follow-up to their unconvincing answer to 'How can you defend those people?' I remain silent.

"You know at the time many lawyers argued they should be committed to the truth even if it meant losing. Trollope does a marvelous job in laying out the argument

"Don't have time. Anyway, I know how it ends.

CHAPTER TEN

LATE FRIDAY AFTERNOON. Jamie's library. I'm starting to feel like a real lawyer, a six-pack, munchies, scattered files, a yellow pad and an open copy of the Evidence Code. Jamie is teasing Rachael about her boyfriend Paul, "Cute, but does he have a job?" Bill is lamenting he has a hearing before Judge Cane, who "never met a cop he doesn't believe."

Sullivan and Myers is representing *Everheat* and has answered our complaint, nothing of interest, just denied everything. Of course we didn't say much in our complaint either. Kept the main allegations, the wrong and the damages, as vague as possible. No use tipping your hand and allowing your opponent to prepare. The details will emerge during discovery. Unless you can keep them hidden. George once told us that Buddha said there are three things you can't hide, the sun, the moon, the truth. Bill, quick to the draw, responded "We're in the eclipse business".

"Looks like Sally Jones will be handling the case," Jamie nervously eyes the Danish.

"I hear she's a bitch." Men don't gossip; they tell it like it is.

"Bill, why's an aggressive male a 'great litigator' while an aggressive female's a 'bitch'?" I steal Jamie's thunder.

"Whatever." Bill shrugs. "Not my issue."

"All issues are your issues except those that aren't." George bites into a pear. We have given up understanding, still thinking about apples. What do they know?

"If we tell Sallie about the assault she might be sympathetic."

"Come on guys, I told you, Sallie's a bitch. You don't get that reputation by being a bleeding heart."

"And you don't make partner at Sullivan either." Rachael adds. They didn't offer her a job.

"I still like my stealth idea. If they know it's coming they might file some kind of motion so that we can't even mention it at trial."

I drift off, as Vicki often accuses. Even if the judge thinks the assault wasn't foreseeable why shouldn't the jury hear about it? Why not let a jury decide if it's 'manifestly unjust' to let Hadley recover his lost profits? Will jurors run amuck? Maybe they have more common sense and a better sense of justice than we give them credit for.

Juries on criminal cases aren't told the sentence if they convict. Jamie had a case where the defendant, somewhat retarded, went into his local convenience store, asked to buy a six-pack on credit, and, when the clerk said 'Sorry', he took out a small pocket knife, waved it and walked out. The police found him sitting outside the store, drinking beer.

Armed robbery, six years.

I resolved to write an article, 'Power to the Jurors, Let the Wild Rumpus Begin'. An extra beer is always dangerous. The valuable and indispensable role of academic scholarship is to challenge the assumptions and practices of the real world. No one else will. They're too busy. Too caught up in the moment.

I might conclude that the current rules are right. Novelists say they are never sure how their book will end. "I never thought she would marry him." Academic writing is like that too. Hard thought might force you to change your initial view but, generally, you come out at least close to where you thought you would. The struggles, the surprises, the joys, are getting there.

And we get paid more.

CHAPTER ELEVEN

"GOOD EVENING. WHAT'S your name?"

"Larry Knowles, Officer."

"I noticed your car weaving. Been drinking?"

"A couple of beers."

"Shouldn't be driving."

"I wasn't. My wife was. My license is suspended."

"Suspended? For what?"

"Drunk driving."

It was a dark and stormy night. No kidding. Officer Sattler's police report:

"I saw a white Toyota driving west on Grant. The vehicle weaved and I followed. It turned into the Speedy Mart at the corner of Pima and Grant. I followed and watched a man exit the vehicle and go into Speedy Mart. He returned carrying a six pack of beer. I approached him asked his name and he told me his license was suspended for drunk driving. His speech was slurred and his eyes bloodshot. I advised him of his Miranda rights and I arrested him and called the DUI squad."

Knowles went online and ended up hiring Jamie's firm. Bill would handle the case.

"The prosecution can't bring up his prior conviction for drunk driving," Bill half asserted, half questioned.

"Not in the guilt phase," Jamie the expert. "But if he's convicted of a second, he's doing serious time. The prosecution will try to get the prior in when Sattler testifies about what Knowles said about his drunk driving suspension."

"I think I have a good Miranda motion."

"Yeah, but you have Judge Cane."

In 1963 Ernesto Miranda kidnapped and raped a 17-year-old Arizona girl. He confessed and was convicted.

"May it please the Court. The conviction of Mr. Miranda should be reversed because when he confessed he was unaware of his right under the Fifth Amendment not to 'be compelled in any criminal case to be a witness against himself.' You can waive that right but one cannot waive a right he doesn't know he has. Police should tell those they arrest that they have the right to remain silent and, unless they do, nothing they say should be used against them. Otherwise the Fifth Amendment is a sham on the nation's streets."

Lawyers, pressed to the wall, come up with wonderful arguments and the Supreme Court bought this one. Earl Warren, the Chief Justice, wrote the Miranda decision. He was the former Governor of California and was appointed to the Court by Ike, rumor has it, as a payoff for some funny business at the Republican Convention that nominated Ike over Nixon. Warren also wrote the unanimous decision in *Brown v. Board of Education*, outlawing school segregation.

At the outbreak of World War ll, he played a key role in locking up the Japanese citizens living on the West Coast.

Even heroes make mistakes.

That his conviction was reversed did not mean Miranda was a free man. It just meant his confession could not be used against him. The cops had other evidence and he was convicted again and sent to prison.

Until someone is in custody, there is no need to *Mirandize* them and anything they say before that can be used against them in trial. Was Knowles free to go when he made his foolish remark? At the pretrial hearing on Bill's motion to suppress the statement the prosecutor called Officer Sattler.

Q: Officer, when you first approached the defendant was he under arrest?

A: No, he was not in custody. I decided to arrest him only after he told me his license had been suspended for a DUI.

Q: So when he made that statement he was not in custody. Nothing further.

Judge Cane: You may cross-examine.

Q: Officer do you believe that my client really believed he was free to walk away?

Prosecutor: Objection. Calls for speculation. This officer has no idea what the defendant thought. And besides it is not relevant.

Judge Cane: Sustained.

Dumb question. You can only ask about what a witness knows, not ask them to guess what someone else was thinking. Bill was actually lucky there was an objection. Unlikely Sattler would answer, "He was shaking in his boots", more likely, "I'm sure he knew he could walk away. I wasn't blocking him and I was conversational."

There was no way Sattler would be the first cop Judge Cane didn't like. Bill tries another approach.

"Your Honor, what the officer thought is not determinative. It is what the defendant believed. My client thought he was in custody, never believed he could simply walk away. Put yourself in his position. Stopped by an armed officer, questioned about a crime. "

"Do you have any cases supporting that?"

"Yes, Your Honor. An appellate decision out of Kansas."

"We're not in Kansas anymore, Toto." Judge Cane thinks he's a great comic; his bailiff, an at-will employee, laughs.

"Motion denied."

Judge Cane is not the first comic on the bench. In Gilbert and Sullivan's *The Mikado*, the High Executioner has a list:

The Judicial humorist, I've got him on the list, they'll none of them be missed.

As to Miranda, he was eventually paroled and, back in Phoenix, well aware of his fame, he made money signing police Miranda cards.

In 1976 a criminal walks into a bar. Miranda was stabbed to death.

Even villains make mistakes.

CHAPTER TWELVE

ARE PRINGLES POTATO chips?

Expecting to debate great Constitutional issues, students are somewhat disappointed to debate potato chips. Few argue *Brown v. Board of Education,* many argue appetizers. (Sorry.)

A statute imposes a high tax on "potato chips". Pringles says, "Don't tax us, we're not potato chips, we're part wheat."

"Well?" I ask my students.

A hand jumps up. "Does the statute have a definition section defining potato chips'?"

"Nice try but no. And no legislative history telling us what they meant. Like prophets, they simply declare things, go home, and leave the rest of us with 'Say what?' When they said 'potato chips' did they intend to cover only things that are 100% potato or chips that are mostly potato and are advertised as potato chips? What do the cases tell us about interpreting ambiguous statutes?"

"The *Brominam* case said that ambiguous statutes should be interpreted broadly to achieve legislative goals. The goal is to raise taxes so 'potato chips' should be read as covering Pringles."

Another hand. "Yeah, but the case we read yesterday said statutes should be read narrowly, and Pringles shouldn't be covered."

Ha! A judicial dilemma! Judges are required to follow prior cases but what if the cases point in different directions?

"There is so much play in the system, so many contradictory rules, the law doesn't control judges. They can decide whatever they want, usually for the rich guy."

This is where my lunch with Ted comes in. He's made that argument. His favorite: The Constitution requires the President be at least 35 years old; a teenage candidate could argue that this requirement was to assure the President knows as much as a person 35 and that she, at 19, knows more than someone 35 did then. (Some arguments are better than others.)

Ted's our Crit. Hair greying, now in ponytails, still going to demonstrations supporting worthy causes. Chanting. Waving fists. I feel guilty. Have I grown up or merely older? Or simply cynical?

In our world the Crits are not gangbangers; they are members of the Critical Legal Studies Movement, the sworn enemies of members of the Law and Economic Movement. So the players are: Law and Economics profs who want the law to promote economic efficiency and return to the early 19th century, the Crits who want the law to protect minorities and return to the French Revolution, and the rest of us, hopelessly confused and wishy-washy, hoping that the law somehow promotes justice or at least fairness. Actually many of us enjoy the intellectual puzzles of the law, whether Pringles are potato chips, and not its politics.

Along with the rest of the university, law schools are accused of being too liberal. Once I asked my AIDS Law class, "If you're gay and applying for a job do you mention it in your first interview?"

"Of course you do," one of my gay students said. "Now it's cool to have a homosexual lawyer on your staff, gay or lesbian, doesn't matter. The people who are discriminated against now are Evangelical Christians."

I think we have one on our faculty but he never mentions it, surely he didn't when he was interviewed. However, even if we are too liberal and even if we brainwash our students it doesn't last. They're hired by conservative law firms. A radical friend told me, "When they hired me the senior partner told me I would be a Republican in a year. Boy, was he wrong. Three months."

Ted and I are at the Student Union, a pleasant walk across the quad, at a corner table away from the bursts of laughter and under-graduate enthusiasm.

"Law protects illegitimate hierarchy." Ted checks out a coed and momentarily forgets the life of the mind. "It's a shell game," he resumes. "tricking the masses, judges manipulate the rules to come out on the side of the rich and powerful. It's all politics."

"Have you ever talked to a judge? Remember Judge Hooker? He quit because the law was making him do things he didn't want to do."

"Yeah, well…. You know things get so much more interesting when it gets warmer and brings out coeds in shorts."

Nothing to argue there. But, after a respectful silence, he reaches for a chip. "But what about the two year proposal? The Dean is pushing it. Needs the tuition money. A way to attract students to our sinking ship. Our first year enrollment was down 20% last year."

"Bad press. High tuition. No jobs. It's not that there are too many lawyers, but too few willing to work at fees people can afford. We could always fill up the class by taking folks with lower LSAT scores but that would kill us in *U.S. News.*"

The *US News and World Report* ranks universities and graduate schools, including law schools. The average LSAT score of your stu-dents plays a big role in your rank. Us professors ignore the rankings safe in the knowledge that popularity is no measure of profundity.

"Those rankings don't mean a thing," we assure ourselves in the coffee room. "Besides we should be a lot higher."

"You don't think they'll cut salaries do you?" The rubber hits the road.

"Come on Ted. It'll reduce income inequality."

"Fuck you. I have a mortgage. Kids. Have you read Mary's new article?"

"Rethinking Employment Discrimination?"

"Yep. Free market crap. Rather than outlaw discrimination let the market do its magic … if you don't hire a terrific worker because of race your competitor will and drive you bankrupt."

'She made an interesting point about *Plessy*. I didn't know it was brought by a railroad. The law required separate cars for whites and blacks and the railroad found it hurt business."

Plessy v. Ferguston held that 'separate but equal' did not violate the Constitution. It was eventually overruled by *Brown v. Board of Education*, 'separate is inherently unequal'.

"So how you going to vote?"

"Probably yes. Piss off the old farts."

"Not to mention your mortgage and kids."

Chapter Thirteen

Over the music, snippets of conversations.

"I thought I was going to flunk out."

"I knew I would."

"I knew what to expect in graduate school. In law school, I hadn't a clue."

"I never wanted to be lawyer. I just wanted to stay in school."

I'm flipping burgers, my only practical skill … get high quality meat. Every summer Vicki and I host a barbeque for our daughters' friends. Feels good to have our big house filled, like the old days. Thanks to Vicki's cooking the place was always filled with laugher and energy, the place to hang.

"Bring your significant other," commanded the invite.

Boyfriend, *girlfriend*, *husband*, *wife* are politically taboo, vaguely suggesting homophobia, and *lover* is a tad much for a party at your parents' house.

Our patio is crowded. Too many tables or not enough. Coolers of beer, cokes and bottled water. A side board with guacamole and corn chips, both ignored by the dieters. The day is sunny. Music, laughter and gossip. Toby works the crowd, appreciating 'nice dog' but hoping for spills. Vicki and I are tolerated, getting several 'do you remember the time?'

Lawyers love to tell horrific law school stories. I loved law school. As an undergraduate you debated endlessly about free will, justice, the good life. Then you went out for a latte. In law school these debates aren't endless, they actually matter, someone wins, someone loses. I loved it.

"No, you didn't. You hated law school," Vicki would say. "Don't you remember getting sick almost every weekend and setting your Criminal Law book on fire?" But one spontaneous act, made by a smoker with a handy Bic lighter, did not prove anything. Besides, it was a Corporations book. I let it pass, content in the knowledge that I *did* love law school.

"Did you keep a list of students dumber than you?" Over the din Rachael's voice carried. "Crossing them off when they said something intelligent. I got down to three. I knew they don't flunk people out but still."

"In my first week," Bill recalled, "I was sitting there, terrified I would be called on. Suddenly the professor calls my name. 'Is negligence a question of law or a question of fact?' I had no idea. Still don't. I just remember the long silence. He was one patient guy. He asked me again. I think he asked again. I couldn't understand what he was saying, except my name. A hundred students turned their lonely eyes and stared, watching one of their flock ripped apart by a lion, thankful it wasn't them. My childhood ran before my eyes." Bill is apt to embellish.

"Hey, I remember that," Rachael said brightly. "I added you to my list and had four."

Paul, a significant other, Rachael's, walked over, bored with law school talk. I liked him. We talked a little baseball. He regretted we didn't have hotdogs. I did too. Gina came over.

I left her and Paul in charge of the burgers and joined the law school crowd.

"Did any of you have Roosevelt for Antitrust?" Jack, tall, fit, was a prosecutor, Jamie's significant other – her public defender friends called it treason.

"Roosevelt was boring, something of a bully. One day he asked this guy to wake up the student next to him. 'You wake him, professor. You put him to sleep.'"

It's deeply gratifying to hear a colleague trashed. Keeping lists is a hard habit to break.

"Remember Professor Hall? At the end of one class, I can't even remember what class, he asked 'What if the dog were an alligator?' My study group spent an hour that night trying to figure out what the hell he meant."

"Yeah, someone wrote that on the blackboard in the student lounge. It became famous. At a Halloween party a couple came as a dog and an alligator."

One of life's big turning points, often unnoticed, is when you start saying "In my day" and go on to suggest in the past things were either much better, or much worse. But really law school is a cakewalk compared to when I was a student.

Fresh from the marches in Berkeley, Cambridge, and Madison, not trusting anyone over 30, a new breed of law professor arrived and the Socratic Method was doomed. Inhuman, inflicts grave psychological damage, teaches the powerful to abuse their power. "We don't want our students doing that to their clients." The rigors of the Socratic Method have been mostly replaced with Socratic Light, students knowing the night before if they will be called on or, still worse, lectures aimed at 'learning outcomes'.

No more sitting in terror, not knowing if you are next, surprised and amazed by professor questions and student answers. Confusion, vitality, excitement, exhaustion.

What if the dog had been an alligator?

I loved it.

CHAPTER FOURTEEN

DEPOSITION TIME. JAMIE is preparing Marie. "Don't worry Marie. We'll be there and all will be fine. Just answer their questions. Just yes or no. Don't try to explain anything."

If you want folks to follow your advice tell them why they probably won't.

"You'll want to explain yourself, make the other lawyer understand your position. Don't. You'll be able to explain later. The other lawyer will never believe your side; she's paid not to."

We're in the posh library of Sullivan and Myers, a large serious room. 14th floor, busy streets below, mountains beyond, long polished wooden table, expensive leather chairs, abstracts on the wall, flowers, cokes and water bottles on the credenza. Although Jamie told her what would happen, and even rehearsed some questions, Marie must be terrified. Thirteen, never in a skyscraper, never seen the City or mountains from way up here. Grownups dressed better than they do for Church. A court reporter asks her to stand, raise her hand, and swear to tell the truth. (Of course, not the whole truth, if she follows Jamie's advice.)

"Marie, I'm Sallie Jones," she's wearing 'Friday casual', not 'litigation killer.' "I represent the *Everheat* company. First let me tell you how sorry we are about your mother and about all that has happened. Our hearts go out to you. We hope we can make things right."

Marie nods. Jamie rolls her eyes.

"Now I sometimes talk a little fast," Sallie smiles, "so if you don't understand a question, let me know. Don't answer any question before you understand it."

"Okay." Marie hesitates, still a little shaky. Jamie warned her about trick questions.

"Are you feeling good this morning? Had your breakfast?"

"Yes."

"Good. And let me know if you start feeling badly. We can stop this at any time."

Call this caring woman a bitch? Surely not.

Sheep's clothing. Friendly Sallie is closing off escape routes, closing doors. Let's say at the deposition Marie admits seeing her mother drunk but at trial she denies it.

Q: Marie, on direct you said you never saw your mother drunk. Do you remember when I took your deposition?

A: Yes.

Q: And you swore to tell the truth?

A: Yes.

Q: Do you remember telling me you saw your mother drunk?

This is known in the trade as 'impeachment with prior inconsistent statements.' How is our poor darling going to escape?

A: Well maybe I said that but I didn't understand your question.

Nope. That door is closed.

A: Well maybe I said that but I wasn't feeling well.

Nope.

Go to a Criminal Court and watch when a defendant pleads guilty.

You'll think that the judge is compassionate, caring. "Are you feeling well today? Had any drugs? Have any promises been made to you about sentencing? Do you fully understand what you are pleading to?" Judges seldom add, "Best of luck, pal, we've got you on record; try to wiggle out of this one."

The deposition went on all morning. School, future plans, that sort of thing.

Jamie just sat there. There isn't much to object about. At trial there are strict rules about what questions can be asked; during discovery, the field is wide open. Sallie can ask Marie about anything that might lead to admissible evidence, such as what other people told her (hearsay), and what she thinks happened (speculation), neither of which would be allowed at trial. The only thing that is off limits is material protected by the attorney/client privilege.

"What did you tell your lawyer about this? What did your lawyer say?"

If everyone shows their cards before trial then settlements will be more likely and trials will be less about lawyer cunning and more about a search for the truth. That was the thinking of those who drafted the discovery statutes.

What's the thinking in the trenches?

"Conceal as much as you can."

Although Sallie was fairly thorough, the sexual assault didn't come to light. Leaving the fancy digs of Sullivan we do our best to project "All is lost" while we were secretly rejoicing. We still have our ace.

What will Marie remember most? Probably the celebratory $12 hamburger. A shock to me too.

Marie has been living with her guardian Derrick Wilson. Things are going fairly well. Marie has even picked up some babysitting money caring for the Wilson toddlers. Thanks to car pools she has been able to continue at the same school but the future is iffy.

Jamie has become quite close to her. She has arranged for Marie to meet with a wonderful woman counselor and drives her to the weekly meetings, stops at Starbucks where she nervously eyes fattening drinks and pastries and recalls happier days when she could eat like Marie. She even helps her with homework.

Before I went to law school a friend of my parents told me, "If you like intellectual challenges, you've love law school; if you like people, you'll love practice."

CHAPTER FIFTEEN

SUNDAY I GO to church, not that I have anything to atone for.

I don't go too often. My parents didn't either but when my sister and I were young they thought it would be good to see if we were interested. For a couple of months we did Catholic, Baptist, Lutheran, Methodist, Mormon. We liked the Quakers the best probably because we insisted on calling it the Crackers. Finally "Well?' We checked "None of the above."

When our daughters were small we took them to Church. They enjoyed the other kids and dressing up. I liked the people. Although they might not read the New York Times, they're solid. Liberal colleagues send money, write letters, attend rallies … church-goers work soup kitchens and take disaster victims into their homes. We would too but our homes aren't set up for that.

I'm not sure why we drifted off. I don't know how many of my colleagues are religious; we never talk religion. For the last several years our family has gone to a Passover Seder at Professor Eisner's. I find it quite moving, reading about the wicked child and discussing whether what happened in Egypt so long ago is playing out today. Admittedly, however, much time elapses between the time we sit down to eat and the first bitter herb and the first glass of wine, thankfully, for us goyim, not just Manischewitz. Vicki's father, who's Jewish and has been to a few, advises 'eat before you go'.

I'm at church to teach, not learn, to convince my audience to go home and talk with their families about possible disability and certain death.

"A talk with your family is more important than a bundle of legal documents." To support our alums I give a shout out for lawyers. 'Don't get legal documents off the internet, talk to a lawyer to make them fit you and your family."

We're in the Sunday-school classroom, about 30, mostly elderly, all visibly uncomfortable in the small chairs.

"Welcome back to grade school." It's good to get a laugh at the beginning. Audiences have no idea how important they are. Had they stared blankly I would have lost all confidence, hurried though my presentation, skipped the jokes, and gone home early.

They would have been the losers.

In my Elder Law class I ask my students if they'd talked with their parents about disability and death. Once a guest speaker suggested I should also ask if they'd told their parents a dirty joke; which is more taboo, death or sex?

"We never talked about death or any of that and when my dad went into the hospital and the doctors asked us about life support, we didn't know what to say. When he died, we felt we'd let him down. It was horrible. We fought over what kind of funeral, about who got his watch, about everything. We've stopped speaking."

I cover the basics, final illness, hospice, bad driving, who gets the grandfather clock. But topics aren't the problem, it's getting the conversation going. Humor helps.

Art Buchwald was dying of kidney failure. A friend asked what he would miss the most. After a long pause he answered:

"Global warming."

I'm open about my discomfort seeing coffins. A couple of my students made a video going to funeral homes. After five minutes of learning prices, guarantees and cremation urns (for golfers), you're on the floor laughing.

A woman, not a day over 80, sits in the front row and nods frequently. A man, a few seats over, laughs at my jokes, even before the punch line. They're like fans lining the street, cheering on marathon runners. I avoid looking at a man in the back who's frowning. Suddenly his hand goes up. I'm dreading "All of this chit chat about talking to your family is well and good but what I want to know is the difference between a traditional IRA and a Roth IRA."

Instead:

"When my mother died the funeral director kept pushing fancy coffins but I said she's dead and doesn't need a fancy coffin. Finally he gave up. In desperation he asked if I would be interested in a nice pillow."

He got the best laugh of the morning. I'll steal it. I just have.

Driving home I consider the flip attitude I had driving over. Maybe I do need some spiritual guidance.

I don't know the lawyers at Sullivan but I'm calling them 'bastards'. The ethics of springing testimony used to bother me but now my only concern is whether we can get away with it. As to suing Child Protective Services, I no longer worry how a verdict will take money from abused and neglected kids. My concern is how we sue CPS without those bastards at Sullivan learning that we have a sexual assault to drop on them.

Will Gina come to believe there are only good guys, scumbags, and violence? Jamie only criminal defendants, horrible prosecutors, and unfeeling judges?

We take a job, wrote Orwell, put on a professional mask and soon our face grows to fit it. He should have added, and probably did, maybe it was implicit, that we should ask ourselves if we like that face.

Chapter Sixteen

ONE OF THE nice things about being at a university is that you can go to talks in other departments. The Psychology Department had a seminar on ghosts. A large number of people have had contact with them, your chances best if you're a democrat and stayed away from college. Despite the movies, most ghosts are friendly, mothers showing up after their funerals to assure that things are fine. A priest was the speaker.

A woman around 40 was in my parish. A few years earlier her husband had died and she was planning to get remarried. Her 18 year old daughter was fine with that, her 10 year old son threw fits. One afternoon, when their mother was out, there was a knock at the door. The son answered it and, after about five minutes, he returned, wiped some tears away and said, "It was dad. He told me it was alright for mom to get married."

That's pretty easy to understand, a man returns as a ghost to make things right. To believe it, however, would mean giving up everything else one believes. So I explained it away with sophomore insights and felt smug.

"Gina, are you taking the detective exam?"

Veggie burgers. Not Toby's favorite. Bi-weekly dinner, this one on the patio overlooking the pool and Vicki's garden. Fresh tomatoes!

"I've decided not to, at least for a while. Remember Maureen, from my Academy class? She was promoted a couple of months ago. Bored out of her mind. Interviewing countless people who didn't see anything, who don't know anything, watching hours of convenience store video of people buying beer but never drawing a gun, reading old police reports. I want to be where the action is. On the street."

"But dear, it's so dangerous." Concern in her mother's voice.

"How about those mini cameras you have to wear?" asks Jamie. "No more shooting unarmed people?"

"Not funny," Gina snaps. A long awkward pause. Vicki asks me to pass the salad, Jamie toys with her fork. Gina realizes a contentious topic would ruin a pleasant evening and smiles.

"Actually they work in our favor. Last month I stopped a lawyer for speeding. He insisted on a hearing. He told the hearing officer how he was rushing to see his dying mother, how abusive and unprofessional I was, yaddy yaddy yadda. Then I was asked what I had to say and I said nothing but that I could play the video of the encounter. Oh forget it, your honor, the guy said, I'll just pay the fine."

"Funny." Jamie asks, "Who was it?"

"David Akins."

"He's an ass. Once he pushed his way into the front of the line at Starbucks shouting 'I'm a law student.'"

"Shakespeare has a great line," me, always the teacher, *"I am Sir Oracle and when I speak let no dog bark."*

"Yep, that's him."

"Lawyers," Gina shakes her head.

"But come on," I'm a tad defensive, "I teach law students. You know what John Adams said?"

"Which John Adams?" Vicki, always the teacher.

"The one who led the American revolution, the second President. He was most proud of his lawyering. He said,

To what higher object can any mortal aspire than to assist the feeble and friendless.'

Two killer quotes at one dinner and I think I got them both right. I risk a third.

"Defending the King's troops accused of murder in the Boston Massacre, Adams told the jury that they no doubt wanted to convict but,

'Facts are stubborn things.'

"He said that?" Jamie asks. "I'll steal it."

Toby moves to Vicki, unaware that she picked veggie burgers. Vicki breaks the silence.

"An interesting thing happened at hospice today, we almost had to call the cops. A long-lost son shows up insisting that Mom go back to the hospital and accusing his siblings of wanting her to die to get her money. Never mind that she's never had much money, that the siblings have gone broke caring for her, and that she's doing better without all the meds."

"People get better?" Jamie is about to hide her half-eaten veggie burger but instead rewards Toby who is always hungry no matter what.

"You'd be surprised. The drugs they take to cure them often interact and make them worse. When we take them away, some even walk out."

"So? What happened?"

"Fortunately mom was coherent. We were able to talk him down but it was scary."

Do I have any drama to add? Any intense human exchanges? Of course most of the cases we study are about people cheated, injured, wrongfully accused, but they're cardboard characters in our search for the law. Occasionally real life does raise its ugly head. First year students go through hard times. All have been academic stars, in high school, in college, and maybe graduate school. Good grades are what they are. Many get their first 'C' from me. Self-images shatter. No joyous calls home. Suddenly average.

"A student who got a C in my class came to my office. Sobbing. 'My parents have spent their life savings sending me here. I'll never get a good job. I've let everyone down."

Vicki, always in search of my compassion, "How sad. What did you say?"

"I told him to cheer up."

CHAPTER SEVENTEEN

"GOOD MORNING, LADIES and Gentlemen of the Jury. I represent Larry Knowles ...."

Twelve men and women, strangers, stare. Am I talking too fast? Too slow? Who should I look at? Am I confusing them? Insulting them by talking down? If only someone would raise their hand, ask a question, even shake their head "I disagree." Anything, but they just sit and stare. What came after the point about it being dark? I don't know how to end this. I'm just repeating myself; I should just sit down. Where should I put my hands? What was my big ending? Shit! They're bored.

"Ah, well, ah, thank you for your attention."

Trials are hard. Doing what you're taught in Trial Advocacy: prepare your questions but listen to the answers, be ready to pivot; never ask a question you don't know the answer to unless you have to; one question, one fact, at a time; don't start at the beginning, start with your second best point, end with your best; personalize the witness but don't bore the jury; stand so the witness looks at the jury, not you; and never, ever, "open the door" by asking a question that allows the bastard to bring in otherwise inadmissible evidence.

Q. So Officer Jones, my client never confessed, did he?"
A. As a matter of fact he did. But because we didn't Mirandize him, his confession wasn't admissible so I couldn't say so on direct."

Then you sit down and your opponent stands, smiles, and approaches the witness. Did she actually wink? Cool and collected. A professor once said that you never look as nervous as you feel. I hope she trips. Shit, I forgot to ask my witness about the lighting. Was my witness believable, come off too rehearsed? Suddenly come the questions.

Are they proper? Do they ask for hearsay? Improper opinion? Do they assume facts not in evidence? Are they leading? Compound? Argumentative? Irrelevant?

That one's objectionable. Should I object?

Will the answer help me? Hurt me? Can I repair the damage on redirect? Will my opponent simply rephrase the question? Will the jury think I have something to hide?

Where is she going with these questions? Will my next witness be here on time? That idiot. Damn, here comes another question.

Next to the prosecutors sit the investigating officers, those who serve and protect, dressed in their spiffy uniforms. The prosecutors, smug in their virtue, ready to pounce on any slip, ready to fudge any line. The jurors, "Well he wouldn't have been arrested if he wasn't guilty," wait to see what 'their lawyer,' the prosecutor, has to say about that and the judge, who has never been to prison, never dropped out of school, looks down.

It's like taking a final every day. Staying up late, rereading the statutes and all the witness statements; new things always jump out. Editing for tomorrow, rewriting your closing. Trying to sleep, "I still have a good five hours."

Yet this is where you want to be. How can you defend those people? How can you not? Walking into a crowded courtroom where everyone hates you. It's just you and your terrified client; there's no higher object to aspire to.

"Yes, Your Honor, I'm ready." Damn right I am.

I'm sitting in the back of the courtroom, no need to make Bill more nervous. Knowles was drunk, no question about it. His defense, he wasn't driving. His wife Sandy will testify she was. On cross, the prosecutor will force her to fess up that she knows if her husband is convicted he'll go to jail, lose his job, and yes, she loves him dearly.

Will the jury believe, beyond a reasonable doubt, when Officer Sattler says Knowles was driving? He's sworn. Good looking. Competent. Trustworthy.

Q: Tell us about the stop.

A: I saw the defendant's vehicle weaving. I decided to follow. He turned into Speedy Mart and exited the driver's side of the vehicle. I pulled in and waited until he came out. He was unsteady on his feet and was carrying what appeared to be a six pack of beer. I stopped him. There was a strong odor of alcohol. I asked him if he had been drinking and he told me he had a couple.

Q: Are you sure it was the defendant who got out of the driver's side?

A: Yes.

Q: But he claimed he wasn't driving. Did he tell you why?

A: He said his license had been suspended.

A long pause and then:

Q: For what?

A: Drunk driving.

The prosecutor turns to the jury with a slight 'Can you believe we're even trying this case?' shrug, and then:

Q: Thank you Officer Sattler. Nothing further. You may cross-examine.

Bill walks to the podium with his yellow pad. Is his theory that Sattler is mistaken or is it that he is lying? A key decision as it will impact on his demeanor. You're not mean to someone who has made a mistake but you better be to a liar – jurors pick up vibes. Bill's conversational.

Q: Officer Sattler, what was the defendant wearing?

From the pretrial interview Bill knew that Sattler wouldn't know. Don't ask a question you don't know the answer to (unless you have to).

A: I can't remember. Maybe a jacket. It was cold. Like I said, it was several months ago.

Sometimes things drop from the heavens. Bill pretend to make a note.

Q: Officer, when did you first see his wife, Sandy Knowles?

A: She came up when I was talking to her husband.

Q: So, you didn't see her before.

A: No sir, I didn't.

Bill pauses, let it sink in. He did not follow up with "So you can't say she was in the passenger seat and not in the driver's seat." Hopefully the jurors will pick that up. Had Bill asked the question Sattler might have come up with a good reason why he could place Sandy in the passenger seat. It might actually be true. Save it until closing argument, when Office Sattler will be long gone, out serving and protecting.

Q: I've been to Speedy Mart. The parking lot is pretty dark. Isn't that right.

I jot a note. That question's improper. Lawyers can't testify. But the prosecution doesn't object; it isn't that big a deal and she isn't a bitch. But if she was a bitch, or bastard for that matter, recognizing that Bill is new at the game, she would object at every opportunity, trying to confuse him. Don Drysdale, the great Dodger pitcher, was asked if he ever threw at batters. "Never, but if you're going to miss, best to miss high and inside."

Q: The car turned left into Speedy Mart, correct.

Questions on cross aren't questions, they're statements of fact to be answered yes or no. Don't let your voice go up at the end of your question, that invites a long response.

Q: And when the defendant got out of the car, you were still waiting to make your turn into the lot. Correct.

A: Yes.

Q; No doubt looking at traffic coming your way to make sure your turn would be safe.

A: I had a good look at the defendant's vehicle.

Q: Is that what I asked you?

By ducking the question Sattler makes it clear why it matters. Witnesses are advised 'Just answer the question even if it hurts our side; if you try to deflect it you make things worse.'

A: There wasn't much traffic.

Q: But your attention would be on your driving, not on the defendant's car. It was about 10 at night, right?

One way to prevent a witness from disputing your assertion is to quickly follow it with another question. Objectionable but things go fast.

A: Around that time.

Q: And isn't I true that Mr. Knowles and his wife are about the same height? And were wearing heavy winter jackets. And whoever you saw was walking away from you on a dark night.

Prosecutor. Objection! Compound question. Argumentative.

Without waiting for a ruling Bill shakes his head.

"I withdraw the question. Nothing further."

Chapter Eighteen

We're in the same fancy library as the deposition. Marie isn't with us. Jamie told me to take off my South Park tie. That hurt. When she was six she had Vicki buy me that tie. I wear it to formal dinners and become a hero to the wait-staff.

"$500,000. *Everheat* won't go any higher."

Jamie stares.

"Look, if anyone was negligent that night it was the mom. If she wasn't drunk she would have walked out. Everyone knows the rotten egg smell of gas; she could have walked out of the room. Frankly we have a good chance for a defense verdict."

Jamie stares.

Being comfortable with silence is absolutely critical. It's never as long as it feels and it puts incredible pressure on the other side to say something, often something stupid. Jamie learned that in countless plea negotiations.

Jamie stares.

Finally: "Maybe I could get them to go a little higher. Do you have any evidence that the pilot was defective?"

"Be serious. Good ones just don't go out."

"They do if they're installed improperly."

"Do you have any evidence blaming Jack's Appliances?"

"You have the burden of proof, we don't."

"We also have a dead mother and an orphaned girl."

There's a great view of the mountains. And free coke. I know how things will go. Sallie will attack our evidence, our theory, our case. Jamie will defend and attack their evidence, their theory, their case. Sallie will defend. Unlike tennis, there is no tie-break. Nothing will be accomplished save some unwitting disclosures. They'll up their offer to a million, Jamie will come down to five million, everyone will shake hands and leave mumbling about bitches.

The Harvard Negotiation Project published *Getting to Yes* proposing a different way, no snarling, no bluffs, no threats, no zero sum. Parties would be honest, candid, exchange concerns, appreciate each other's position, make the pie bigger rather than fight over who gets the bigger piece. Numerous examples were given proving wonderful results. Not to be a cynic but it's child-play to come up with examples that support your thesis. Been there. Done that. Still the book became a rage at the law schools, it promised a kinder, gentler way to practice law. Professors have always been uneasy throwing their graduates into the contentiousness of the career they had happily avoided.

I actually saw something like it work. Law students were roleplaying a negotiation. An elderly widow, whose husband recently died, was suing an insurance company and the fight was about how much it should pay. The first half hour was traditional - each side ridiculing the other.

"You can't prove that!"

"Can too!"

"Can not!"

Then, out of the blue, "How much does she need to live?" The students got on the same side of the table, listing expenses, estimating costs.

Making threats, exploiting vulnerabilities, are verboten in *Getting to Yes*. Jamie had not read the book, at least not carefully.

"Sallie, talk to their sales department, not the legal. Even if you win, no one will remember 'badly installed,' or 'drunk mom'. They'll remember *Everheat* furnace kills."

"This won't be news. No one's going to pick it up."

"Really? *Everheat* furnace kills wife of war hero. Leaves 13-year-old daughter homeless. News at 10. We'll pitch the cables."

"That's unethical! I'll report you to the bar. Get a gag order."

Jamie is calm. We had rehearsed the bomb.

"*Everheat* kills mom. Gets judge to silence victim."

Sallie stares. It's not true that opposing lawyers, deep down, like each other. "This is going nowhere. See you in court."

We shake hands, walk the to elevator, mumble about bitches.

CHAPTER NINETEEN

"Remember me?"

"Of course I do," even if you don't. Kudos from the development office. You meet alums at annual dinners, airports, basketball games. It's always nice to be recognized, particularly if you're with friends. Occasionally it's a little awkward.

"You know, Professor, you said something I'll always remember."

Should I ask? I usually do, always optimistic, hoping it was pithy, profound, poetic, perhaps John Adams on assisting the feeble and friendless, George Orwell on faces and masks, or even Shakespeare on barking dogs. Nope. It's always trite, incomprehensible, usually both. I've learned to smile and change the subject.

Still it's always good to be reminded how important teachers are in the lives of their students. Last year I ran into one my students, now a very successful lawyer.

"I was about ready to drop out but you told me I could write well. No one had told me that before. I stayed."

I didn't remember that. It's scary to realize that a casual comment might make a big difference in someone's life. What do I know about life? "Hey, guys, just because I didn't say your comment was brilliant doesn't mean you're a defective person. I'm not a role model. The only thing I excelled at was taking law school exams."

When Jason phones I recognize his voice immediately. He'd been a student in my Contracts class. We were studying the Statute of Frauds which requires that some contracts, not all, be in writing. He raised his hand.

"Professor, I have a question about the Statute of Frogs."

Instant hero. Now he's with the State's Attorney General's Office.

"Prof, see you're slumming with us mortals."

"Good to hear from you, Jason."

After a little small talk, "Anyway I've been assigned Marie's case against CPS. Your case isn't that strong. She never reported the sexual assault. I've talked to the foster parents. She had a crush on Mike, maybe a case of unrequited love. And I talked to his case manager at CPS, Robert Thor. Says he's a decent kid, kinda shy, doesn't think he would assault anyone."

"Marie is pretty strong on what happened." I don't actually know if this is true but the situation seems to dictate a minor mis-statement. A little wrong to do a great right.

"Not saying it didn't happen. The trial would be a mess. It won't be fun for Marie."

He offers $20,000. "Tops" without talking to folks "higher on the food chain." Something about grandmothers and buses. It's a good offer. I promise we would get back to him soon.

"Cool. Like you used to say in class, 'If you can't swim, don't walk on old bridges.'"

I never said that. I cover quickly.

"So, Jason, how do you like practicing law?"

That night's dinner, tofu that supposed to taste like meatballs. I prefer veggie burgers, Toby prefers meat, no matter the risks and aren't there always new studies?

"Jamie, what's with Rachael? She seemed out of sorts at yesterday's meeting."

"Paul dumped her."

"Frailty, thy name is man." I can be irritating.

"I had a long talk with Paul at the party," says Vicki. "Very nice young man. Smart, seems to have good values, well-read. Prefers Dickens to Trollope. But one has to be concerned. Almost 30. No real job."

"You're way wrong," Gina jumps in. "He has a good part time job at the University. Information technology. And is almost done with his Master's."

Apparently they got along at the picnic. "That's nice, Gina. Jamie, how's Marie?"

"Holding up. I've been helping her with her math. She's doing better."

"That's funny, you tutoring math. But that is really nice." Despite their posturing my girls have great affection for each other.

"I'm worried about Marie. What will happen if she wins millions?"

Jamie looks at her mother, puzzled. "What do you mean? Be happy."

Gina adds, "You read about people who win the lottery, quit their jobs, have nothing to do. Friends, even those they didn't know they had, ask for money. Booze, drugs, Vegas. A girl with millions will always suspect that her boyfriends are after her money."

"Men are always after something." The girls laugh, Vicki frowns. "So I throw the case?"

"Why not?"

"*Why not?*" Jamie looks at me as if I'm slow learner. "Because you're a lawyer, not God."

"Shouldn't a lawyer do what's best for their client? Maybe that means looking at the long term rather than the short term."

"I'm sure Marie wants to win. You do what your client wants."

"Oh come on," I'm irritated. "You know full well that lawyers can almost always get their clients to do what they want them to."

"Look, I care deeply about Marie," Jamie stares at me. "I'm losing sleep over what's to become of her. Sure I can convince her what to do. That just means I have to decide and it's a bitch."

Never once, in all my years of teaching, did I have such responsibility.

CHAPTER TWENTY

IT WAS A good morning. We learned Judge Castro will be the trial judge in Marie's case. A year ago she was acting as a Juvenile Court judge. A clean-cut teen, about 15, was standing before the bench.

"Before I sentence you do you have anything to say?"

He did. A great deal. He had been doing a lot of reading. About the causes of teen rebellion. About the destructiveness of drugs. About the teenage mind and how it had yet to develop understanding of long-term consequences. He has learned a great deal about himself, about how to cope with his bad attitudes, he has learned his lesson and will never get in trouble again.

"Are you done?"

"Yes, Your Honor."

"Do you expect me to believe that crap?"

The boy's mother ran toward Castro. The bailiff jumped, prepared to stop an assault,

"Thank you so much," she sobbed. "My son is so smart, so good looking, so charming, he's able to talk his way out of trouble. He gets away with everything. I know if he keeps getting away with it, he'll end up in prison."

Insightful mother.

Judge Castro will not put up with any crap from Sullivan.

More good news. "Not Guilty City! The jury was out only an hour. Let me tell you how I got the cop!" Bill was joyous.

We took him to lunch, Rock and Roll Diner. Crowded, corner table, Chicken Fried Steak with extra gravy. I listened to the tale he would tell over, and over, and over.

Lawyers don't need Super Bowl rings, only an occasional victory.

"The state's expert got away from you on cross."

"Yeah, but I won, didn't I?" Bill resented me raining on his parade.

"If you want to win again, focus on what went wrong, not right. When I got out of school I worked for California Rural Legal Assistance in the San Joaquin Valley. Our client, Manny Noriega, a maintenance worker, was fired by the City Manager of Delano. He claimed Manny wasn't doing a good job. Our theory was that he was fired for his union activity and we appealed. Guess to whom?"

"Superior Court?"

"Nope, to the Delano City Council. Fat chance, right? Anyway Gary Bellow, my supervisor and the best lawyer I have known, handled the hearing and, miracle of miracles, he won. We all went out for beer and high fives. You know what Gary's first question was?"

I waited. One of life's most important lessons deserves a couple of seconds.

"Why did the City Manager get away from me on cross?"

No day stays good. Back at the office we found a fax listing the witnesses Sallie plans to call.

"Looks like they'll raise mom's drinking. They're calling the pathologist."

"Damn. How bad was it?"

"Extreme."

"It's a bluff," Jamie always the optimist. "Risky to attack a war widow, a woman they killed. Might backfire."

Might not.

If you find that it is more probable than not that the defendant Everheat Manufacturing, was negligent, you are to find for the plaintiff, Marie Cadnum.

A rather low bar, a 'preponderance of the evidence,' not 'clear and convincing' or 'beyond a reasonable doubt.' Still our case is thin.

We do have a very sympathetic plaintiff but jurors take their oaths seriously. They won't blow off the negligence question. We have the statement of the regional director, which he will probably deny, and one from a local dealer who had discontinued that model of *Everheat* furnaces because of pilot problems. Not that strong a witness; Sallie will suggest he's just covering himself because he installed the furnace improperly.

Things would be easier if we could convince Castro that we didn't have to prove negligence, like in the case of the missing sponge. If so all we would have to do is prove up our damages and throw a little dirt on *Everheat*. But Rachael is coming up short in her legal research so we can't count on a favorable ruling.

But all's well that ends well. About 6 in the evening, as we were all heading out, the phone rang. An altered voice:

"In *Everheat's* files, the ones turned over to Sullivan, there is a memo from McCoy concerning new patents for the furnace. You will find item 9 quite interesting."

Click. Buzz.

CHAPTER TWENTY ONE

"Yes," Sallie says in her 'Oh hum another boring morning' voice. "There's a memo from McCoy."

Call's on speaker. No one moves.

"What!" Jamie's voice, covering a smile, shocked and outraged. "And you didn't send it over?"

"Didn't have to. In your Demand for Documents you asked for all documents showing that *Everheat* may have known of the trouble *before* the incident. The McCoy memo was sent several months *after* the incident."

"You can't be serious, Sallie. That's a clear violation of the rules of discovery. I should report you to the bar."

"I sent what you asked for. Bad drafting on your part. My job isn't to bail you out."

"What does item 9 say?"

"I'll fax it."

Twenty minutes later. A celebration! The smoking gun!

9. Before submitting the new patent application take a close look at the pilot mechanism. On recent tests it has suddenly turned off, leaving gas escaping.

Bill, master of metaphor, "We got them by the short hairs." But who sent it? I turn to George. "George?"

"Bad karma."

"Sallie?" Bill shrugs.

"Lawyer does the right thing," George says. "Film at 11."

Max Weber, and it was Max Weber, said that a teacher has a *moral* obligation to raise the 'inconvenient facts' that lurk in everyone's position, not to talk them out of it, but to slow them up. Sometimes students confuse our motives. "So," I ask, "disregard the rules if it will lead to a good result? Ends justify the means?"

George is serious. "Martin Luther King said you can break the law if you do so lovingly and openly, willing to take the punishment."

"Forget who made the call. Sallie violated the discovery rules for sure. Her excuse is bull. Should I report her to the state bar?" Jamie is troubled. She has an ethical obligation to report, but she admires Sallie, a bitch standing tall among the bastards.

"She didn't rat you out for saying we'd seek press coverage," Bill supplies the excuse ... and the editorial.

"I'll hold off." Jamie concealing her compassion in cunning. "It's good to keep your ace until you need it."

Bill laughs. "Two wrongs, one right. Violate discovery and make it up by violating client/attorney." I leave for the law school.

The long-awaited faculty meeting. The first order of business was whether to hire a director to create a clinic for students to represent veterans. The University allots only so many faculty slots to the law school so it would come down to a Vet Center or a new professor in the fast developing field of intellectual property. It was a close vote but liberal guilt carried the day. Now our students can serve those who served, much better than "Thank you for your service."

I think a big factor occurred a few months before. As part of a 'Get to Know Your Fellow Students' program, some talked about going to war. Since the military has gone all-volunteer very few of us even know a soldier and know virtually nothing about war; it's more complicated than kicking down doors and hugging four-year-olds waving flags on airport runways.

"Every hour of every day, for seven months, someone was trying to kill me. That's why I sit back of the room -- no one can get behind me – and I jump if anyone drops a book and I have a hard time concentrating on what the professor says."

"The best things in my life and the worse things happened in Iraq. Often on the same day. I would go back in a minute except for my leg."

"I would never go back. I killed two guys in a car. Felt really macho shooting them. But we can't just leave them there. Have to 'tag and bag'. Looked at the driver. My age." He bit his lip, struggled, and tearfully "He probably had a son like I do."

A small petite woman stood. "I was in a truck going to Fallujah. An IED exploded and the next thing I know I'm on the ground, bleeding badly. I thought I was dying. That I would never see my parents again. I was making my peace with God but my comrades were there, keeping me conscious, offering their support, I knew they would die for me and me for them.

"I never felt so safe in my life."

Welcome home. Rather than dying for each other we're more likely to yell at each other, politics, religion, race, guns, and rather than supporting each other we compete against each other, grades, jobs, money, and prestige.

She'll never feel that safe again.

CHAPTER TWENTY TWO

"CHOICE. STUDENTS SHOULD be able to graduate a year early."

Mary, the darling of the Law and Econ tribe what with her article on rethinking employment discrimination, leads off; the traditional mantra, 'Let my markets go!'

"Many students owe over $100,000 and this will allow them to start their jobs a year early. Besides there are many people out there who want to become lawyers but are supporting and raising their families and can't take three years off. This will allow them to fulfill their dreams."

Legions of moms and pops pining away, I hadn't heard that one before. Probably Mary came up with it on the way to the meeting. Often the good reasons we have for doing what we're doing come to us after we're doing it.

The faculty seminar room is used as the lunch room when, against our better judgments, we resolve to get along better, to share not only cutting edge ideas but also tuna sandwiches. At faculty meetings it's crowded, with most of us rubbing elbows, sitting at the long conference table littered with coffee cups, some ostentatiously editing their most recent article for publication, the world waits on pins and needles. Portraits of prior deans stare down, becoming less stern as the years progress. I've told you things are getting easier.

Grace McVane, our first woman dean, sits at the head of the table, her blue business suit reminding us all she's just returned from fund raising, her main job. Faculty summer grants hang in the balance. As a secretary in a law office she decided that she was as smart as any of the lawyers. Those smarts, and her ability to take shorthand, propelled her to the top of her class at Berkeley. She was new and doing a great job; her only flop was the faculty lunch program; free tuna sandwiches don't always work.

Mary doesn't address why students incur such large debts – it's impolite to talk about our high salaries, salaries that are 'necessary' to meet market demand. "Do you know how much they make at UCLA?" Never "Do you know how much they make at Legal Aid? Or at Grossmont High School."

The two-year option is a way to attract students in the face of falling enrollments. The rest is filler.

"This doesn't make any sense. This will decimate our clinical programs. We're criticized for not preparing our students for practice and we respond by turning them out a year earlier. We just voted to start a Veteran Clinic but with half the class graduating after two years we won't have enough students to run it."

"Look, I voted for the clinic. I'm as patriotic and compassionate as you are. Are you seriously suggesting we hold our students hostage for a year so some vet can get disability?" Things do get testy.

"Jay, will this work?"

Jay is the associate dean. He keeps the place afloat. We may not agree on much but we all agree he's simply terrific.

"Yep. We will have to offer three courses in the summer and a couple of short courses during the Christmas break. We make up tuition lost in the third year with that from summer school and the short courses. It's revenue neutral."

A collective sigh. No matter what, our salaries are secure.

"Sounds like a forced march. They'll miss the intellectual life of the school, clubs, speakers, Law Review."

"Come on. This isn't the death of clinics or law review. Most students will stay for three years."

"Maybe, but this will send a message that we're a trade school. Not a place to reflect on law and the profession but a place to get through as soon as possible."

"Students have concluded that already. Haven't you noticed how many third-years skip class so they can clerk for lawyers downtown?"

"So we throw in the towel?"

"Now that's an idea, let's make law school two years for everyone. The third year is a waste." Ted's comments are particularly hurtful. Law profs love the institution. Why not? It told us we were special, anointed, smarter than the average bear. Tinker yes, attack no. The unkindest cut of all came when Obama said he thought law school should be two years. We even had bumper stickers!

"Few of us practiced law," Ted twists the knife.

True. Most law profs come directly from the top of their class at a top flight law school. Rather than practice law, many clerk for a judge, some even at the Supreme Court. As law schools become interdisciplinary, profs with advanced degrees in economics, psychology, statistics, are the hot item.

"If you do divorces, prosecute crooks or even advise sharks on corporate take-overs, do you really need to know about the affirmative use of collateral estoppel, covenants running with the land, or the minority rule concerning *per stirpes*? What you need to know is how to read a case, interpret a statute, ask good questions. If we can't teach them that in two years, a third won't matter."

"Ted, where have you been? We're not teaching the affirmative use of collateral estoppel. We're using legal doctrines to teach legal analysis, judgment. Struggling with hard legal problems makes them smarter, makes them better lawyers."

The Dean asks for a show of hands. A few are a tad slow, seeing who was voting for what. It passes, 16 to 9 and students can now graduate in two years. Hopefully it'll trigger serious discussion about what we, as an institution, hope to accomplish. Most of us take our classes seriously and work hard to make them better. However there is little thought of how one's class fits with others to accomplish the school's overall mission.

Whatever that might be.

Learning law, although it doesn't seem that way, is the easy part. I sat in countless classes struggling to learn laws I knew I'd never need. *Quasi in Rem jurisdiction?* Give me a break. What's the point?

I found out the summer after my second year. Like many law students I went South. James Chaney, Andrew Goodman, and Michael Schwerner had been murdered but, being young and immortal, there was little fear.

I worked for a Civil Rights lawyer in Albany, Georgia, C.B. King, one of only two black lawyers in the state. The summer before he was beaten by the sheriff; years later they named the federal courthouse after him. Albany was hot, muggy with roaches, otherwise wonderful. I lived with other law students in the black area of town, everyone was friendly and accepting of out of town whites, some writing stories, some registering voters, some caring for kids in the new childcare center, all singing "We Shall

Overcome." The hand fans did little to keep sweat from your eyes; they advertised funeral homes.

The Voting Rights Act had been signed by Lyndon Johnson. It took real courage for blacks to register to vote; everyone knows who you are, where you work, and where you live. Soon after I arrived there was an election in a small town, Americus, about 50 miles from Albany. It was for Justice of the Peace. For the first time, blacks were voting. Their pride and enthusiasm were shattered when they got to the polling place.

"Whites Vote Here"

"Coloreds Vote Here"

"I want to file suit to throw out the election and make them do it right." C.B. gave me the case. Big mistake. I knew nothing about election law. C.B. had his own law library; they wouldn't let him use the County Law Library. I looked up cases dealing with elections tainted with illegal voting procedures, mostly from Chicago, mostly involving dead people.

"No luck, C.B. The cases are against us. Before a court will void an election it must be shown that the illegality affected the outcome. In our election it didn't. Jennings won by a very wide margin."

A cold stare. But C.B., I'm law review. I slinked back to my cubby. A monkey could've found those cases.

Sitting in class, I thought I was learning gift tax and property; I was really learning how to read cases, spot ambiguities, parse language and construct arguments. In short I was learning what I needed to know in Georgia.

Back in my cubby I managed to figure out why the cases that I thought spelled our doom didn't and, in fact, found language in some that supported our position. I wrote a memo.

"So Mary Lou Hammer wasn't making any trouble, just standing peacefully in line, waiting to vote, yet you arrested her for being in the wrong line. How did you know she was in the wrong line?"

C.B. had filed a habeas corpus in federal court to get her out of jail and to have the election thrown out. On the stand was the deputy sheriff.

"How did I know she was in the wrong line?" he smirked. "I'm not completely color-blind."

In 1896 Justice John Marshall Harlan wrote:

"The Constitution is color-blind." We underlined it. Twice.

Thanks in large part to C.B.'s brilliance, and a tad to my memo, the Judge ordered the release of Ms. Hammer, voided the election and ordered a new one.

Weeks later I drove with C.B. to see the new election. He took the dusty narrow road – longer but deserted. In high school I did little, mostly unsuccessful, drag-racing, but I never realized how terrifying speed can be: a black man driving a white boy was simply an invitation to a pickup truck and a broad smile, "What you doin' boy?" I sat in the back seat, ready for rednecks and blow-outs.

When we got to the courthouse, one line:

Vote Here.

Suddenly I knew: the law is not something to learn, the law is not something to argue, the law is something to do.

Chapter Twenty Three

"Rapport? Gimme a break. I'm not a social worker. My clients call me 'Mr. Wilson.'"

Should lawyers have clients call them by their first names? Becky thought yes, Mr. Wilson, no. David, who teaches interviewing, and I were putting on a Continuing Legal Education Program for the Public Defenders. A large well-lit room, student type chairs with desks, about thirty lawyers, some in suits, some in jeans, but most in between. Desperate to fulfill their yearly continuing education requirement, they would even put up with us, provided there's pizza.

I recalled the early days of Legal Aid and the debates about proper dress. In 1965, Lyndon Johnson declared the War on Poverty and funded legal services for the poor. Recent law grads, fresh from the War on War, wearing jeans and sandals, flocked. Having won the "I'll never work for a big firm" the battle shifted to "And I'll never dress like them." They met the stern stares of lawyers who had been Legal Aid lawyers before Legal Aid was cool.

"Poor people deserve lawyers who look like lawyers. And, for God's sake, take that flower out of your hair."

"*Mister* Wilson," one of his colleagues responded, "It doesn't matter what they call you as long as they believe you care. People have to know you care before they care what you know."

What a great line. *People need to know you care before they care what you know.'* I'll steal it. Students might write it down, remember it. Make me proud at alumni dinners.

"Professor, remember me? I was in your class. You said something I'll never forget. There was something about clients caring you know, but the one I remember was the one about the old bridge."

"Caring," Mr. Wilson responded, "very cute. Good advice if you're a social worker. We're lawyers. I don't want to be friends. These people are criminals. My job is simply to get them the best deal I can."

"But when you have the 'Come to Jesus' talk, unless they trust you, they won't believe you."

'Come to Jesus' is short for sitting your client down and explaining that pleading guilty now and getting two years is better than getting ten years after trying to convince a jury that the butler, on one of his days off, did it.

"If they don't take my advice, end up doing a lot more time, I couldn't care less."

"We're social workers, at least some of the time," argued Becky. "Last year one of my clients, a prostitute -- I spent hours helping her get back into school. Ran into her this morning. She turned her life around and is working at my Starbucks. Gave me a free latte. Getting married."

"Speaking of 'Come to Jesus', do you just lay out alternatives or push what they should do?" David asked.

"In law school," shot a voice from the back, "we learned about client centered lawyering or something like that. Only spell out alternatives, clients decide. Yadda, yadda, yadda." It was Caleb, one of Jamie's favorites. I recognized him from TV; he had a lot of high profile cases. "If we let our clients decide the prisons will be even more overcrowded."

Laughs.

In the 50's the lesson was different. Lawyers should simply tell clients what to do, no questions asked, no reasons given. "If you explain you'll just confuse them and maybe get in an argument." But lawyer-as-prophet couldn't survive Question Authority, Self-Esteem, and Informed Consent.

"Informed consent? Doctors, after scaring you with all the things that can go wrong, won't even tell you what they would do if it were them."

"I read a study. Most patients want doctors to tell them what they would do instead of just sitting there. Put some skin in the game."

"I tell them to take the plea. And I don't have any skin in the game."

Client autonomy doesn't mean the lawyer stands mute. If the client wants to pave paradise and put up a parking lot, "How will you feel about it in a couple of years? What will your kids think of you? What happens if you run into Joni Mitchell?" A famous corporate lawyer, whose name escapes me, said that more than half of a corporate lawyer's job is telling clients what they couldn't, or shouldn't, do.

"Say your client tells you he is guilty but insists on a trial. You can't let him testify but should you try to convince the jury, not only that the State hasn't proved its case, but that someone else did it? Should you cast guilt upon the innocent?"

"Professor, cast guilt upon the innocent. Great idea. I'll try it."

Laughs.

"I'm serious."

Caleb, from the back of the room, "In ethics we read about some English lawyer who said your only obligation is to your client and that you must do everything you can for him even if it brings down the nation."

It was a Lord addressing the House of Lords in 1821. I assign the article. A lawyer must do everything for the client, 'reckless of consequences, though it should be his unhappy fate to involve his country in confusion.' That extreme position was controversial then as it would be now. But the author, Professor Mellinkoff, nails it:

> *The lawyer is no sweet kind of loving moralizer. He assumes he is needed, and that no one comes to pass the day. He is a prober, an analyzer, a decision maker, a compromiser, eventually a scrapper, a man with strange devotion to his client. Beautifully strange to the man-in-trouble; ugly strange to the untroubled onlooker. But the man-in-trouble is you, I, and our neighbor at the right moment. The lawyer, some lawyer, is there for each of us.*

CHAPTER TWENTY FOUR

"No FURTHER QUESTIONS. Mr. Evans, please step down." The lawyer turns and walks back to his seat.

A nervous hush falls in the courtroom. Mr. Evans squirms on the witness stand, fidgeting, desperately trying to figure out what to do. He can't walk, his leg lost to medical malpractice. When he took the stand his lawyer took his crutches back to counsel table.

Silence. Seconds feel like minutes. Without looking up from his papers, his lawyer repeats, "Mr. Evans, please step down."

The jurors are aghast, transfixed. Someone help him!

Thus was born the personal injury revolution. No more "It's hard getting around with one leg"; now it's sitting on the witness chair squirming. Lawyers made the injuries real, jurors felt the pain, and huge verdicts followed.

"Marie's necklace with her dad's Purple Heart will be a killer. When she's testifying, have her take it out, and then ask 'What's that?' and wham, slam dunk!"

We're talking strategy, making plans. Jamie's library, same crowd, same refreshments.

"Bill, it can't come off staged. Marie always wears the necklace and will probably fidget with it while testifying. Then I'll ask her, out of the blue. Her answer will be spontaneous, real, believable." Jamie is a hell of a trial lawyer.

"What should she wear?"

"I'll take her shopping. Something on the young side. Something suggesting grief. More than one outfit or would it be more moving if she had to wear the same one every day?"

"Who's going to prepare her?" I reach for a Pringle.

"Rachael will take her through some cross." I don't envy Sallie. Crossing a kid is risky. Juries resent bullies. Too bad Sallie isn't a six five, overweight man with a booming voice.

"As to direct, I'm not worried that she'll freeze. She held up during her deposition. Sallie didn't kill the Queen; she made her stronger. Before she testifies I'll simply remind her of the areas I'll go over. Her background, plans, the death of her father, finding her mother. I won't rehearse it; I don't want it to become stale."

An actor comes to the director. "On opening night, when I asked for the butter, I got a great laugh. Tonight, barely a giggle. What happened?"

"On opening night you asked for the butter, tonight you asked for the laugh."

I love that story, tell it often. When I repeat it, it seems to lose its punch.

"In what order? Start with the trauma of finding her mom or with how things went badly in foster care?" The best trial lawyers read novels to learn how to tell good stories.

"Haven't decided. Start strong, finish strong. I'll put the less compelling stuff in the middle, like her plans for her future. Although it's all good."

"It was the best of times, it was the worst of times. Why couldn't Dickens make up his mind?" Bill sips his beer, smiles, an 'A' in staff meeting.

"Dickens must have been into Zen," muses George.

Testimony can be terrific theatre. "Remember how Marie told us that every birthday her mother woke her up and read Dr. Seuss's *Birthday Book*? I'd end it there, leave the jury with the image of her mother sitting on her bed, reading the book."

"Yeah, Dad, I saw you almost tear up when she said that. What about the mom's drinking? Should I draw the sting?"

"Draw the sting," advise trial experts. "Bring up the bad stuff before your opponent does, suggest that it isn't that big a deal, brush it aside."

"Oh, by the way, before I forget, before you were arrested for littering, you committed, oh yes, let's see, treason."

But even if you draw the sting, your opponent can still bite.

"You expect us to believe telling the British where John Hancock is hiding is no big deal?"

Rachael hits the real problem. "Sallie pays a price if she brings up mom's drinking. Jury might resent her for trashing the woman they killed. If we bring it up first, by drawing the string, then Sallie has a free pass to attack."

"Let's lie in the weeds," always Bill's first choice. "Don't mention it. If Sallie brings mom's drinking up on cross, on redirect, Jamie can ask Marie when her mom's drinking started. 'When the two Army soldiers came to our apartment and gave her a flag.' Compelling."

"You should go to Hollywood. But with your looks you should be leading man, not directing."

"Jamie, you're not the first one to suggest that."

"Is the illusion the screen or the audience? Or both?"

I ignore George, putting at peril my understanding of the universe. "Speaking of movies, remember Bill Murray in *Ghost Busters*? He told his crew that he had one rule, never have sex with a ghost. Later he meets an extremely attractive ghost. Reminded of his prior pledge, he said 'That wasn't a rule, it was more of a guideline.'"

"So?"

"So? Treat the advice of experts as guidelines, not rules."

Rachael, always sharp, "Is that a rule or a guideline?"

Beer, wine, and chips fuel debate and pithy sayings, but are not so good for maintaining focus. Without resolving the sting issue, at least I don't think we did, we're talking about Sullivan's last offer, $1.5 million.

"Bill, what's your take?" He's been studying reporting services that list current jury verdicts and been talking to lawyers experienced in the field. Lawyers love to give advice.

"Well, I found a recent case where two sisters, about Marie's age, sued for the wrongful death of their father. Medical malpractice. Both had been placed in foster care. The jury came back with $6 mill. That's three mill a piece."

"We might do better than that," says Jamie, "our plaintiff is very attractive and, what with the smoking gun memo, *Everheat* looks sleazy."

"If we don't do better than $1.5 million we'll have to pay *Everheat's* litigation costs and that would pretty much bankrupt the firm." Rachael takes a sip from her coke. We glare. People only *purport* to love the devil's advocate.

"What do you mean?" asks Tower Man.

"Dad, it's a device to encourage settlements. If a defendant makes a low ball offer, there is no pressure on the plaintiff to settle. However, if the defendant makes a good offer, then there's a lot of pressure. If we don't get a bigger jury award than the offer we pay."

"Like baseball arbitration," Bill adds, "the arbitrator must pick either the player's offer or the team's ... no splitting the difference. Both sides know that if they take an extreme position they'll lose, the arbitrator will have to pick the more reasonable offer."

Beer, wine and chips affect people differently. Some crash into depression while others soar into the bright blue. We're the lucky ones: raising our glasses, we soundly reject the *insulting* offer of Sullivan.

"Should Marie testify about the assault?" Leave it to a coke drinker like Rachael to sober us.

"I'm torn," says Jamie. "She's reluctant but it might help her to tell what happened. No longer a deep dark secret. No longer something to be ashamed of. There is a lot of literature suggesting that going public is therapeutic."

"And add another million," toasts Bill.

"But what if the jury doesn't believe her? They might call Mike and, if he denies it, the trial becomes a 'she said, he said' contest. Don't we want to keep the focus on our case, on her mom's death, not on a sexual assault?" Rachael opens another coke. She deserves it.

We don't resolve that one either. But I leave happy, recalling my favorite couplet:

Malt does more than Milton can,
To justify God's way to man.

CHAPTER TWENTY FIVE

"TO DO A great right, do a little wrong."

"Leave it to Dad to quote *Merchant of Venice*," Jamie butters a second dinner roll, thinks better of it, and reaches under the table to grateful Toby.

"Don't be hard on your father. It's the only play he knows. And don't talk with your mouth full."

"Mother, it's your fault, your good cooking. You're turning Toby into a vegetarian."

Little did she know of our walks by McDonald's.

"Thank your grandmother. Both of you should learn. I know, busy career women. I took time to learn how to cook. I was a career woman before there were career women."

"Yes, Mom, you've mentioned that before." It's not that us seniors forget we have made the same point, told the same story, again and again; it's just that we have a limited number of them.

"Any plans?" If you're unwed at Jamie's and Gina's ages, when your mother asks "Any plans", there's no need for clarification.

Jamie responds. "Jack and I are still going out but no, mother, no plans." Gina acknowledges she is *seeing* someone new but, to avoid follow-ups, quickly changes the subject.

"A guy I work with stopped a car and found a lot of cocaine and a gun. Major felony. But the stop was bad, didn't have reasonable suspicion, just a hunch. The perp's lawyer is going to get the arrest thrown out unless my friend makes up a good reason for stopping the car. What do you think?"

"Is this 'My cousin wants me to buy him this *Playboy*'?"

"Let me guess, he pulled over a black guy?" muses Jamie.

"No. You're such a racist.... an Asian."

"Well, I'm sure the cop will lie, do a little wrong as Dad says."

"I wasn't endorsing that. I was showing off. Remember Bev Steel? She used to be a Public Defender. She's now a judge and hears cops every day. She tells me she's surprised how honest most are."

"Not in my cases."

"Do a little wrong," Vicky cautions, "and bigger wrongs get easier. Portia despite her wonderful talk about the 'quality of mercy' forced Shylock to convert to Christianity."

Actually it was the Duke but never correct an English teacher.

Gina doesn't share my reluctance; children can get away with more than spouses. "In Shakespeare's time forcing someone to become a Christian was a good thing. Got them into Heaven." To reward herself Gina has another helping of pasta salad and smiles wickedly at Jamie.

"Dad, what was that quote about your interest affecting judgment?"

"A man's interest distorts his judgment more often than it corrupts his heart. I tell my students that but they never write it down."

"Too many words," Gina, at the ready.

"You may be right about the forced conversion," acknowledges Vicki. "But Shakespeare did give all the good lines to Shylock. That shows what a great writer he was, understanding the despised aren't one-dimensional. I'll talk to Dorothy about it. She knows

Shakespeare. She's a new patient in hospice. Taught English at the University. Sad. She's suffered unnecessarily. Her family called too late."

Mortality is more of a downer than perjury. I'll have to talk to the kids, get my affairs in order, maybe after the trial. Finally Jamie breaks the uncomfortable silence.

"I have to pick a jury tomorrow. Any ideas?"

"Defense lawyers want minorities and people who work with their hands, prosecutors want Prussians, bankers and, in a bind, Rotarians."

"Funny, Dad, but stereotyped. What are Rotarians?"

Yet another 'You're getting old' reminder; not only do police and doctors look like they're in high school, they don't even know what Rotarians are, not to mention those guys in the funny hats.

"Rotarians died out with the dinosaurs. You've heard of *them*, haven't you?"

"Don't get testy, Dad. I heard something on NPR the other day." I never stereotype, but Gina's probably the only cop to listen to NPR. Maybe George did, the first small step before his tumble (his word) into enlightenment. "They said women take a broader view of things while men tend to focus on specifics. Women might think in terms of Marie's life without her mom while men might focus on why the pilot went out."

"You should have gone to law school."

"Too many words," Jamie smiles at her sister.

"Does it really matter who's on the jury?" I ask. "Judges tell me that juries almost always get it right."

"Yeah, well, you never know. Last year there was a guy I just knew would be a prosecution juror." Jamie pours herself another glass of wine, half a glass. "He became the foreperson and they acquitted my guy."

"Bill Buckley said that the first hundred names in the phone book would do a better job running the country than the Harvard faculty."

"Tell that to George. This isn't helping. I have a jury to pick even if it doesn't matter and despite the views of fucking Bill Buckley."

'Fuck' is okay in our family. It's the new 'Gosh'. I think I've told you that already but I've only so many stories.

Each side tries to rig the jury. Pre-emptive strikes, few in number, can be used to excuse jurors for any reason, except for race.

White juror: I think he is probably innocent but I can't get over the fact he was carrying a gun.
Black juror: I grew up in a neighborhood like his. Almost everyone carries a gun to protect themselves.

Any number of jurors can be challenged for cause: they know the parties or seem biased.

"Try to get people who hate corporations and like giving money away," suggests Gina.

"What about jurors who've lost their parents when they were young? Wouldn't they be sympathetic to Marie?"

"That's dangerous, Mom. I don't want a one-person jury. Someone who might say 'I lost both my parents when I was Marie's age and no one gave me a million dollars. Sure, it was rough for a while but I survived; made me stronger.'"

Fuck, the real world is more complicated than I thought.

"I'm a big believer in vibes. I'll involve Marie. She'll get a good sense from how the person looks at her, how they respond to questions. Her guess will be as good as mine."

Lawyers get to question, voir dire, prospective jurors. The official purpose, to unearth bias. Off label, to preview their case and, apparently, to trigger vibes.

"The law allows for pain and suffering damages. Do you have any problem with that?"

"If the evidence shows that Marie is entitled to several million dollars in damages, would you award that amount?"

"I got a question for you," Gina jumps in, "If Marie had suffered the slings and arrows of outrageous fortune, would you give her a pound of flesh?"

An 'A' in family dinner.

Chapter Twenty Six

"JUST GOT A fax from Sallie. Two million."

Morning before trial. Coffee and donuts replace beer and pretzels, tension replaces calm.

Jamie shrugs. "What do you think?"

No one wants to go first and take a position, but I'm more uncomfortable with silence than most. "Close call. We could lose on the liability issue and get nothing."

Rachael isn't wishy-washy. "I still think we can convince Castro to give us a jury instruction that we don't have to prove negligence. If she doesn't, we have the smoking gun memo. So I think we'll be okay on liability. They must too if they're offering two million."

"Just to play devil's advocate," Bill, not wanting to take ownership, "I think they have a strong case. First, mom drinking. Even if their furnace was bad, nothing bad would have happened if mom was sober, she could have walked out. And, as to the memo, they'll have their experts testify that if the furnace is installed right, the pilot works perfectly.

Silence. Fidgeting. We look at Jamie. A relief pitcher, the bottom of the ninth, a field goal kicker, two seconds on the clock, a surgeon, lifting the knife.

"Fuck it. I'll recommend to Marie that we turn it down. I'm not going to let her down. She needs to tell her story, to confront those self-satisfied bastards who killed her mom. Trials are more than about money."

Uncertainty vanishes. We rally. We're ready. Damn right!

That afternoon finds us in Judge Castro's chambers, drinking coffee, nervously asking about families, talking some politics. Informality can be deceptive. There's a court reporter poised to type.

Rachael is trying to convince Castro a bad pilot is like a forgotten sponge. Key ruling.

"Your Honor," begins Sallie, "a pilot going out is in no way comparable to a sponge being left in a stomach. There is simply no way for a sponge to get there unless the doctors were negligent. There are several ways for a pilot to go out without the negligence of *Everheat*. The furnace could have been installed improperly, a repairman might have made a mistake, there could have been a problem with the gas line. The plaintiff is suing us for several million dollars for something she says we did wrong … but now wants you to tell the jury she doesn't have to prove it."

Castro nods, "I think you're right. Motion denied. What do you have for me?" she asks Sallie.

"An instruction telling jurors to ignore how much her mother would have made over her lifetime. Wouldn't have gone to Marie."

Some motions are made to be denied, to create an appealable error in case you lose the trial. Never smile and thank the judge who makes a reversible error. Judges can always change their minds.

"Denied. You can argue that to the jury. Drink up. See you in the morning. And professor, it is always good to see you. I didn't realize you had a suit."

Sallie has her appealable issue even if, in the long run, it's a loser. An appeal can take years and Marie wouldn't get the money until it's over. Most plaintiffs are willing to take a cut in their judgments. If the verdict is really out of whack, a hot coffee at McDonald's, a judge might tell the delirious plaintiff:

"Calm down, Dude. The verdict is really weird. Unless you agree to take less, I will declare a mistrial and we can start all over."

The trial team has dinner at our house. Jamie brings Marie. She's very smart – she thanks Vicki for the wonderful brownies -- but she's not too interested in what professors do all day, or lawyers for that matter, but George, George keeps her enthralled with tales from his days on the force. Us too.

CHAPTER TWENTY SEVEN

"LADIES AND GENTLEMEN, you have only one thing to decide."

What is Sallie doing? Instead of going to the podium she walks and stands behind Marie who sits with us at counsel table, the chair closest to the jury. Judge Castro sits regally on her raised dais, the one with the large golden state seal. She looks surprised. Says nothing. Below her, the court clerk, busy with paperwork. In the well, the court reporter with his steno machine. The bailiff, friendly and overweight, sits to the side. Bill, Rachael and George sit behind us along with some friends Jamie asked to come to make it look like there are a lot of folks on our side. A couple of suits from Everheat showed up but Sallie told them to go home. Visuals matter.

Marie is dressed in her school uniform. Nice touch. In her opening statement Jamie focused on the trauma Marie has suffered and will suffer. Two jurors wiped away tears; all looked at Marie, some slowly shaking their heads. She's too shy to make eye contact making her even more in need of their rescue. That wasn't coached.

Jamie didn't mention the sexual assault not wanting to tip our hand if we decide to go with it and if we don't, it would come back to bite us. Sallie takes notes. In her closing argument she would argue, "Remember in her opening statement counsel said Marie had been sexually assaulted? There was no mention of the sexual assault in her case. Counsel was simply trying to inflame you."

While we think we have a good case on the liability issue, Jamie stayed away from it in her opening. We decided to focus the case on Marie and not on *Everheat*. Besides we wanted to see how Sallie would play it, perhaps blame the installation or even Marie's mother. What we weren't expecting was this.

"A tragic accident," Sallie looks at the jurors. "We don't know what went wrong, maybe the installation, but *Everheat* will not contest liability. We want to make things right for Marie."

What is this shit?

"How much will it take to assure that this fine young woman lives a full and rich life, becomes the doctor she wishes to be, joins the Army as did her brave father."

Using our own ammunition against us. Bitch!

"Plaintiff's lawyers will try to make this trial about an evil, uncaring corporation."

Damn right we will! Sallie turns from the jury and takes a long accusing stare at Jamie. Jamie tries hard not to look guilty, or pissed. The jury always watches.

"This trial's not about punishing *Everheat*. That will not help Marie. Don't let plaintiff's lawyers confuse you, play to your emotions. Listen to their witnesses. But ask yourself, why is this witness testifying? To convince you to punish *Everheat*? Or to help you do what you have to do, make things right for Marie?

"Marie will never be made whole. But we can do as much as possible, as much as is humanly possible. How much money will it take? That's the question you must answer. The only question you must answer."

Pause.

"She'll need counseling. Best available. She'll need support through high school. Tutors to help her catch up. She'll need money for clothes, books, meals."

Sallie slowly walks to the podium looking back at the audience. She turns to the jury, seems lost in thought.

"How about college? Medical school? Tuition, books, rent, and spending money. She'll need a car." It's as if she just thought of these items rather than having practiced the words, the pacing, the timing. Bitch.

Pause.

"Make a list. *Everheat* will pick up these expenses. $300,000? $500,000? A million?"

Pause.

"Plaintiff's lawyers will ask for millions more. Millions won't bring her mother back. But what will millions do? Rob her of her drive, of her ambition. Why go to medical school when you have millions? Marie has been robbed of her mother."

She stops. Looks slowly at each juror individually. In a low voice: "Don't steal her dreams."

Wow! Now we're the bad guys. Brilliant. Bitch.

Sallie had been in my AIDS law class. She was a very good student. First in her family to go to college, she went to law school planning to work with kids. Her kid brother got involved with drugs and went to prison. Before graduation she dropped by my office.

"I really want to work in Juvenile Court. I know I can help save kids like Joey. But Sullivan has offered me a job. Everyone tells me it's a great job. I'll be the first woman in the firm, unbelievable pay. I'll learn a lot, get a handle on my student loans. After a couple of years I'll quit and work with kids."

"After three or four years, I'll do what I want to do."

Saddest words in the English language.

At least Sullivan requires its lawyers to do pro bono, volunteer at legal aid, Habitat for Humanity. Sallie volunteers teaching kids locked up in Juvie. She also teaches Sunday school. "The kids in Juvie pay more attention and some are really bright. Love being asked their opinions rather than being lectured at."

"Call your first witness," Castro runs a tight ship. No time to regroup in light of Sallie's startling opening; no time to curse the bitch. Jamie calls Pat Lopez, the first EMT on the scene.

Yes, the apartment was filled with gas; yes, she feared fire; yes, there was a woman on the couch. No, they couldn't revive her, and yes, there was nothing they could do. By drawing out her questions Jamie is able to keep Pat on the stand until it's time for lunch. Time management, while not up to NBA standards, is crucial.

Jamie's office. Beer stays in the frig. Subway sandwiches. "Why didn't you object to Sallie's opening? That was argument and you don't supposed to do that."

"I froze. I knew I should object but didn't know what to say. I'd look like a fool. Fuck it. Where do we go from here? She killed us."

"Fuckers," Bill's at a loss for a good metaphor. "If we go after *Everheat* we'll look like we are beating a dead horse." Like I said, Bill's at a loss for a good metaphor.

Chapter Twenty Eight

IN THE AFTERNOON session Jamie calls Dr. Mathews, our expert, dressed 'Interesting, but Lovable, Professor' –tweed jacket, khaki pants, bow tie - red. He teaches Econ at the U. He testifies about the mother's lost earnings, the projected education expenses, and the projected living expenses, well over two million. And we still have 'pain and suffering,' our big items, to go.

But cross is a bummer. Always is. Billed as the best way to discover truth, better than lie-detectors, and even better than the old way, throwing people in lakes to see if they float.

"Say the jury agrees with you," Sallie begins her cross, "and sees the damages over the next 20 years to be two million. Should they just award the two million?"

"No. They would have to reduce that to present value."

"That's right. Better to have two million today than two million twenty years from now. If you had two million today and invested it, you would have in twenty years, what, eight million? Ten million?"

"That would depend on interest rates, inflation rates, market fluctuations, and a host of other factors."

Jesus. Why not "Maybe"? Is there no limit to pomposity?

We're off on a long confusing ride. I'm not sure what the jury got out of it other than two million today is worth more than two million tomorrow and that experts are incapable of giving a straight answer, lovable or not.

Finally! Dinner with the team.

"Mike refused to talk to me."

On the way back from lunch we had spotted Mike sitting outside the courtroom. Was he here to testify? What would he say? Jamie sent George to talk to him. Long shot. No luck.

George is having a salad. Surprise. "Doctor told me to lose some weight." Neither Jamie nor Rachael, both experts on losing weight, tell him Caesar salads are not the way to go. Buddha, despite his great wisdom, had nothing to say about losing weight.

Obviously.

"I don't think we should go with the sexual assault." Bill has rethought his idea of calling Mike and have him take the 5th. "Marie doesn't want to testify against him and we shouldn't put her through that."

"Going soft on me?" teases Jamie. "I'll tell her she wouldn't have to testify as to the assault. It's great they won't contest liability. We have a strong case but one never knows. Why do you think they did it?"

"My guess," I say, "is that *Everheat's* main worry is bad publicity. They know they're gonna lose but if we show they knew the risk but still sold their furnaces, that could really hurt them. Jamie's threat of the cable shows coming home to roost."

"The only thing you know is what you don't know."

I turn to George. I don't know if I'm annoyed or amused. "When you said stuff like that when you were a cop, what did the others do?"

"They loved it. Cops have a much better sense of humor and a much better understanding of the folly of human existence than you guys who turned your homework in on time."

I'm enthralled. The sense of community, of shared purpose, and, frankly, of fun. It's so much better in Jamie's library than in the faculty lounge. Professors, bless them, are a tad competitive (an A in faculty lounge) and, because they are working on their own projects, there is no sense of shared purpose. Academics are the new monks; rather than spending long days copying ancient manuscripts, they sit before their computers producing ancient manuscripts.

No, that's not fair. A great deal of academic writing is invaluable, advancing human knowledge and giving new ways to think about old problems. Still, outside the monastery, life is in 3D and color, excitement, movement, defeats and victories, bitches to deal with and clients to console.

And yet. The freedom. There are no 'To Do' lists. No one tells you what to do. Time to read an interesting article or to write about something that excites. Something you read, something a colleague said, or even something you thought, will explode in your mind. You get up early, skip breakfast, anxious to get to the computer.

Tolstoy wrote that we have only two questions, what to do and how to live. Too late for me?

Chapter Twenty Nine

After both Jamie and Sallie rest the Judge gives the jury instructions. They are long, boring, and confusing. We all try to look interested.

Ladies and Gentlemen, it is a good idea not to express a strong opinion at the beginning of your deliberations as you become an advocate rather than a judge. It is best to listen to your fellow jurors before you come to a decision.

This makes a great deal of sense, but lawyers don't want judges, they want advocates. The question is how to recruit them. Some pound winning points into their heads, talking too long, repeating the obvious, and boring everyone to tears. The more subtle approach is to scatter clues, leave bread crumbs, so that the jurors think they have discovered the winning points on their own. They'll be damned if they'll listen to their fellow jurors.

Sallie scattered clues. When the pathologist testified she established that Marie's mother had a high alcohol reading. She didn't make a big point of it but, before her next question, she paused to allow the jury to reflect. Without attacking the victim, and paying the price that would entail, she planted a seed, (If she hadn't been drunk this wouldn't have happened).

Planting seeds puts Jamie in an awkward position. Should she take it on directly?

Ladies and Gentlemen, the fact that Marie's mother had been drinking does not mean she could have saved herself.

Maybe the jurors hadn't thought of that and now they would. But if they had thought about it, Jamie would have to offer good reasons why the mom's drinking shouldn't matter. Litigation ain't easy.

After the smoke clears I'll take Sallie to lunch. At the end of the year, Zelda, who runs our Child Advocacy Clinic, will retire. Sallie would be an ideal replacement. I'll try to get her interested and maybe, just maybe, "So, Sallie, who leaked the memo? I thought it was heroic."

Ladies and Gentlemen, it is your duty to follow the law as I give it to you.

We don't want jurors wandering off the Res. Was a time when lawyers could argue that the jury should ignore the law. In Colonial America a sure winner,

"It's the King's law. Don't enforce it."

You can no longer argue jury nullification, no more "This law is unjust; don't convict." Of course "If the glove doesn't fit, don't convict" still works.

The PLAINTIFF has the burden to prove, by a preponderance of the evidence, that the defendant was negligent.

That seems rather straightforward but it conceals important policy debates. If we want to favor victims we could rewrite:

The DEFENDANT *has the burden to prove that it was not negligent.*

If we wanted to give defendants more protection:

The plaintiff has the burden to prove, by CLEAR AND CONVINCING EVICENCE, *that the defendant was negligent.*

These policy decisions are not self-evident nor set in stone. Maybe our way isn't the best.

Visited Old Bailey in London. Robes, wigs, no Rumpole. The judge sums up the evidence, "The Crown points to X while the defense answers with Y." I feared it might be skewed in favor of the Crown but it wasn't. Seems better as it helped the jury sort though things.

The trial had gone without hitch. As *Everheat* had admitted liability we didn't get bogged down with competing experts. We decided not to offer evidence of the concealed patent memo partially to avoid the 'dead horse' response but mostly to avoid a series of witnesses *Everheat* would call to prove the memo was not as bad as it appeared. Keep the focus on Marie and her damages.

Marie was a terrific witness. She relived, not simply retold, coming home and finding her mom on the couch. "Mom, wake up. Wake up!" She described her life before, sad because her father had been killed, happy with her mom, her friends, her school, her future.

Jamie's last question: "What will you miss the most about your mom?"

Marie didn't know this was coming. She looked down at her hands, finally, in a low and tentative voice:

"Her sitting on my bed, reading to me. Doctor Seuss. Harry Potter."

You weren't even there and still a tear.

What about the offer in our case against Child Protective Services, $20,000? Can we still accept it? When Jason made it he believed that Marie would testify about the assault. Now it's clear she won't. An experienced lawyer, before he wrote the check, would ask if anything had changed in our case. We might hem and haw but the truth would eventfully come out and the offer would be retracted.

But Jason wasn't experienced. Do we have an obligation to bring it up? Something to discuss.

The necklace worked out better than we could have staged. She took it out when Sallie was cross examining her. On redirect Jamie asked:

Q: Marie, I noticed you had something in your hand. What was it?
A: My father's Purple Heart.

Bill had nailed that one.

Trials are excitement, adrenalin, focus, movement, argument, small victories, small defeats and then, suddenly, it all crashes, stops

Ladies and Gentlemen, now it's your turn. Follow the bailiff back to the jury room. He has the verdict forms.

Waiting for a jury to return is sitting in the doctor's office, waiting for the result of the biopsy, skimming old magazines, trying to look calm, confident. Suddenly the nurse calls your name.

How long will they be out? Did you see the juror in the back row cry when Marie was on the stand? Yeah, but the guy next to her was frowning when Jamie made her argument. Think we have time to go back to the office? I'm worried.

Two days later.

"This is Judge Castro's clerk. We have a verdict."

We rush back to the courthouse. If the jurors look at you when they walk in, good news. If they don't, a crushing blow, it's all been in vain.

"We the jury, duly empaneled in the above entitled matter, find for the plaintiff in the amount of $3,700,000."

CHAPTER THIRTY

BEFORE THE GIRLS arrive at our celebratory dinner I grab a glass of wine, sit by the pool, hit the Opera App, and watch the sunset. Sure, there's terrorism, poverty, but still our species has come pretty far since crawling out of the slime, sitting by the pool, drinking wine, listening to Verdi, watching the sun flash behind clouds. Toby, chewing on her Victory Bone.

In high school we thought the perfect way to die would be having sex. Good news, death was not around the corner, bad news, neither was sex. My current choice is Rigoletto, fading light, and cheap Merlot. What do I have? Four, five good years. Maybe I should take up Yoga. A student wrote a paper on the virtues of elder exercise. One man was thrilled when he could, once again, put his pants on standing up. Good for him ... but it struck me then, and it strikes me now, 'Enough already'. A time should come when there are no more accomplishments, no more knee bends.

A time to simply be.

And yet, why not finish my Contracts book? Better still, why not throw it all in and burn my candle at both ends?

Over *La Donna E Mobile,* Vicki's voice, "Dinner! Light the candles."

Light the candles?

A suggestion from the cosmos? But at my age, come on, how do I burn candles?

Toby and I are greeted by a festive table. Our best china, cloth napkins, candles. I can't believe my eyes, Toby can't believe her nose - steak.

"How did you like the real world, Pops?" Jamie pours a glass of the $15 Merlot she brought for the occasion. No lawyer has ever spent more than $20. And Jamie never calls me 'Pops.'

"Offering me a job?" I lift my glass.

"What grade did you get in Crim Law?"

"Don't remember. But I loved it."

"You hated it. You burned the book." Vicki, wrong but consistent.

A slight involuntary shake of my head, read by Toby as "Probably no steak for you" and she has been such a good dog.

"I'd give you an easy case. Knowles was arrested again."

"He must have your number on speed dial," muses Gina. "Some lawyers are suggesting that. Robbing a bank? Put our number on speed dial, things might go badly."

"Where have you gone, Atticus Finch?"

Mashed potatoes! They more than make up for Vicki's faulty memory.

"Was his wife with him?"

"Nope, That's why it's easy. No one could win this case so it doesn't matter if you screw up. I'll have Bill help."

Bill? Help? A voluntary and vigorous shake. Toby, now convinced, moves to Vicki.

"Sallie called. They won't appeal if we agree to $2.5 million. I told her MSNBC wants to interview Marie. Sallie didn't even bother to threaten a bar complaint and went to $3 million."

Let's think about that. After Jamie's fees there will be way more than two million. Put it in trust to pay for Marie's living and educational expenses. She wouldn't get the rest until she turns 40. Not too long to wait. Vegas will still be there.

There was some bad news.

"Rachael's leaving."

"Paul?" I ask.

"No, she's over that. He actually started dating someone before they broke up."

"That would be me," Gina looks down.

"No shit?" Jamie's silent, stares at her sister. Finally, a big smile, "That's wonderful, Gina. I always liked Paul."

Excitement. Apparently this is serious. Vicki is delighted to hear Paul wants a family and can't stop talking about how IT is the wave of the future.

"Just don't get married before me," cautions Jamie. "I don't want to end up as a character in a Jane Austen novel."

Vicki smiles, thinking of all the nights she sat on beds.

As to Rachael, we learn she grew up in Phoenix and got a great offer from one of the leading firms, Lane and Associates.

"Pops should write a novel." Vicki, a great kidder, stresses 'Pops'. "You're always going on about how books write themselves, quoting that popular author, what's his name?" She stresses 'popular' and smiles at her joke.

"Stephen King. He never plots; says our lives are plotless. But you need some idea what your novel is about. They don't spontaneously combust."

Gina, ever helpful, "I have an idea. A law professor teams up with his glamorous daughter to try a wrongful death case."

"No one would be interested in that." All concur.

"Coming to the office for tomorrow's meeting? We still have to decide what to do about suing CPS."

"I'll be there. Trader Joe's has $3 Merlot."

"Why don't you move into Rachael's old office?"

"I dunno. I've really enjoyed the field trip. I'm reading a novel and a character is described as an explorer, not a hunter. Maybe that's me."

"Hunters dress better," Vicki, ever hopeful.

"After the excitement won't it be boring, sitting before your computer, typing away?"

I think about that. Great question. "Nope, not boring. You chase suspects, I chase ideas. Capturing a vague thought, teasing out its implications, dealing with its dodges, with counter arguments, with sentences that just don't work, and finally getting it right, finally understanding what I mean."

"You know the Supreme Court referred to one of your Dad's articles and adopted his reasoning."

Both girls agreed, "Way cool!"

"It was a minor point. Not to change the subject but I've been thinking and we have some important things to discuss. Have you heard about Art Buchwald and global warming?"

"Oh God," Gina laughs. "Not that. We've all heard your 'need to talk about death' spiel."

"At least 500 times," Jamie nods.

It's good to bring your daughters together, even at your expense.

"Okay," Gina concedes, "Cremation, burial, feeding tubes. Great way to end a festive meal."

"You're right. I guess it can wait for a couple of weeks."

The table's cleaned, the dishes washed, and the girls leave. Toby and I go out for more opera. Full moon, reflected on the pool's water. Toby loves to swim and takes a late-night dip. She eats like a vacuum cleaner, she swims like, well, like a dog.

Maybe it's the wine, maybe the steak, but I'm anxious to get to the office. So much to tell my students, so much to debate with my colleagues, so much to think about, so much to write about. Bill springing testimony, George going incognito, Sallie abusing discovery, I'll reread Trollope and consider a lawyer's obligation to the truth, and what about that kid? Maybe it was his Dad and not some Freudian static. Maybe there really are more things in Heaven and Earth than are dreamt of in our philosophy.

I'll take George to lunch.

Fuck the eulogy. I'm an explorer.

ACKNOWLEDGEMENTS

ONE SHOULD START with one's high school teachers even though it's too late: Mary Smith, Mrs. Hall, D. Smith, and George Gross. And then the profs at Boalt who introduced me to the wonderful world of law and then C.B. King, Dennis Roberts, and Gary Bellow who taught me how to do it.

Robert Hegland, Bill Boyd, Adam Friedlander, Candy Terrell, Mary Ann Presman, and Barbara Sattler spent hours working the manuscript. And thanks for suggestions and encouragement to Caleb Hegland, Alex Lane, Sherina Cadnum, Sarah Lovett, KD Elkins, Nini Lee, Charlie Hegland, Larry Durbin, Lynne Mucci, Ben Sattler, and Meg Park.

Finally, and mostly, my wife, Barbara Sattler, who was a criminal defense lawyer for 17 years before becoming a judge and, drawing on those experiences, she wrote two terrific books, *Dog Days* and *Anne Levy's Last Case,* and has a completed manuscript in search of a title. "You get antsy if you don't have enough to do," she told me. "Write a novel."

I give a lot of advice. Best by far: *Listen to your spouse!*

(An earlier version of this novel was published as *Law Prof.*)

54725092R00083

Made in the USA
Columbia, SC
04 April 2019